Successful Negotiating

Letting the Other Person Have *Your* Way

Successful Negotiating

Letting the
Other Person Have
Your Way

By
Ginny Pearson Barns, Ed.D.

CAREER PRESS
3 Tice Road
P.O. Box 687
Franklin Lakes, NJ 07417
1-800-CAREER-1
201-848-0310 (NJ and outside U.S.)
Fax: 201-848-1727

SUCCESSFUL NEGOTIATING
Cover design by Barry Littman
Printed in the U.S.A. by Book-mart Press

To order this title, please call toll-free 1-800-CAREER-1
(NJ and Canada: 201-848-0310) to order using VISA or Mas-
terCard, or for further information on books from Career
Press.

Library of Congress Cataloging-in-Publication Data

Barnes, Ginny Pearson.
    Successful negotiating : letting the other person have your way /
by Ginny Pearson Barnes.
        p.   cm.
    Originally publisher: 8 steps for highly effective negotiation.
Shawnee Mission, Kan. : National Press Publication, c1995.
    Includes index.
    ISBN 1-56414-359-7
    1. Negotiation in business. 2. Negotiation.   I. Barnes, Ginny
Pearson. 8 steps for highly effective negotiation. II. Title.
HD58.6.B38   1998
    658.4'052--dc21   98-5754

Contents

Introduction

"Jack Sprat could eat no fat
His wife could eat no lean
And so between them both, you see
They licked the platter clean"

—Mother Goose Nursery Rhymes

Jack Sprat and his wife had different needs, and meeting them required negotiation. The nursery rhyme leaves you believing that they were both satisfied. Like Jack Sprat and his wife, you want to come away satisfied when you negotiate. Despite your differences with others, it *is* possible to have successful negotiations.

Thinking about the word "negotiating" may conjure up images of tough labor union confrontations. Maybe it reminds you of the last time you tried to negotiate a deal on the sale of your house or request a salary increase. If it was a difficult experience or you lost, then negotiating seems negative. How successful you've been determines your reaction to the process and the word "negotiating" itself.

In reality, negotiating is something you do every day at home, in your job, in your community, and in the marketplace. Any time you tell someone that what you want is different from what they are giving you, you're negotiating. You negotiate when you return an item you're dissatisfied with to the store. You negotiate when you discuss parameters of your teenager's use of the family car. You negotiate with your spouse when you plan a family vacation. Sometimes you get what you want and are pleased. Sometimes you're not satisfied and are angry, frustrated, or unhappy.

Negotiating can be positive or negative—it can have winning or losing outcomes. This book shows you how to negotiate successfully. You'll learn the secret of how to get to a win-win situation, where both parties come away feeling satisfied. Only then can negotiations be effective. If only one party is satisfied, then the situation or conflict has not truly been resolved.

Successful negotiation can't occur without successful communication. Chapter 4 offers many techniques to improve your communication skills on the road to becoming a more highly effective negotiator.

This book is also about relationships. Chapter 3 focuses on how relationships affect your negotiations. When you negotiate, you do it in the context of a relationship—you do not negotiate by yourself. When you have an ongoing relationship with someone, your success in negotiating is frequently determined by the depth of the relationship. The quality of the relationship affects the negotiation, and the way you negotiate affects your relationship.

This book will describe eight steps to successful negotiating. When you use the eight steps, you'll satisfy yourself and others. And when you are satisfied, you've negotiated successfully.

Eight Steps to Negotiating Successfully

1. Unravel the mystery of negotiating.

Take a positive view of negotiating and toss away the myths you've created about the process. No longer is negotiating negative or mysterious. You can define negotiating, look at how it happens between people, and understand what it means to win.

2. Understand what drives you and others.

Negotiating is needs-based. What you ask for and the way you behave when you negotiate are based on your needs. It's important to look at what you want and why you behave the way you do, and to then see how you can reframe what you're asking for to meet your needs. You must also identify and understand others' needs better. This includes understanding and being able to make statements about beliefs, attitudes, values, and feelings.

3. Learn to celebrate differences.

Here you learn to "put on another's shoes" and create a positive attitude about the person and relationship. Celebrating these differences requires a positive attitude. The celebration of differences in negotiating involves using specific words and behavior.

4. Negotiate with honor, knowledge, and understanding.

Communication is an important part of negotiating. Body language communicates more than words. It tells others how much you like them and how you see yourself. It's important to recognize the meaning associated with certain behaviors and then to build continuity between what you say and what you do. Being able to apply the Four "Cs"—Care, Clear, Comprehensive, and Calm—forms the foundation for maintaining the dignity and respect of both parties.

5. Do your homework before negotiating.

Negotiating effectively means being prepared. How do you research and prepare to be successful? First, *mentally* prepare by deciding to create a successful negotiation, then *intellectually* prepare by choosing the appropriate strategy. Last, *emotionally* prepare by using self-talk to create a positive self-image before you enter the negotiation.

6. Negotiate actively, honestly, and fairly.

The negotiating process has six stages. They include asking questions, making affirmative statements, framing, listening, reasoning, and reframing. With each stage it's important to stay principled, separate the person from the problem, focus on common interests, and reinforce commitment.

7. Create a champion from a naysayer.

Difficult people sometimes seem impossible. They stand in the way and tell us "no" for reasons we don't understand, or they may be obnoxious, harassing, or highly controlling. We must understand why people behave in difficult ways and learn to use three magic phrases to neutralize difficult behavior: "I agree," "I respect," and "I appreciate." We will practice the four strategies that stop difficult behavior.

8. Create satisfaction with your outcome.

It's much more fun to win than lose. It's easier to be satisfied when you've won, but winning comes with both short-term and long-term payoffs. You need to view negotiation as a process, not a one-time event. Part of this process is to learn from and stay positive at the end of each negotiation.

These eight steps prepare you for success, help you during the process, and let you evaluate the outcome. The eight steps are also meant to inspire, to help you be better at what you do every day. We'll follow each step chapter by chapter in this handbook, answering questions, suggesting tactics, and building negotiating confidence as we go.

Chapter 1

Unravel the Mystery of Negotiating

What Makes Negotiation Tough?

Negotiating can be intimidating, frustrating, and overwhelming. Yet when you look at the dictionary, the written definition of the process appears simple. Negotiation is give-and-take between people or between people and organizations. To negotiate means to bargain, to make arrangements, to settle with someone. It's the art of reaching agreement through an effective exchange of information.

Put into practice, though, the process becomes more difficult because negotiation usually involves give-and-take about a disagreement. While definitions are clear and objective, disagreements often involve emotions and subjective perceptions. Therefore, communication is an important part of negotiation. We must communicate what we want clearly and unemotionally and listen to what the other person wants.

Negotiation also seems more difficult because the disagreement occurs *within a relationship*. You don't disagree by yourself, you disagree with others. You don't bargain by yourself, you do it with others. For many people, disagreements result in only one thing: confrontation. To reap success at negotiation, you need to work on the relationship that exists between you and the other party as you negotiate and put aside the notion that disagreement automatically means confrontation.

With this in mind, we can expand our definition of negotiation to its application in real life by saying:

Negotiation is the resolution of a disagreement, using give-and-take within the context of a particular relationship. It involves sharing ideas and information and seeking a mutually acceptable outcome.

Developing successful negotiation requires:

1. Learning the process of negotiating.
2. Understanding yourself.
3. Building better relationships.

If any one aspect is ignored, then negotiation will be less effective.

In the 1950s, *The Burns and Allen Show* was a popular TV comedy. One evening, as the show was closing, George Burns asked Gracie Allen to give the audience her famous recipe for beef pot roast. She gave the following instructions:

"First I light the oven. Then I take a small beef pot roast, salt and pepper it, place it in a small pan, and put it in the oven. Then I take a large beef pot roast, salt and pepper it, place it in a large pan, and put it in the oven alongside the small roast. The secret is, when the small roast is burnt, I know the large one is cooked to perfection!"

While we might shake our heads at Gracie's antics, many of us would admit that we often feel like the burnt roast in our disagreements. While others are ensuring that their roast is "cooked to perfection," we're getting burned.

Negotiations don't have to be like that. Whether you disagree with a performance evaluation, or your spouse wants to take a different vacation than you, or the community wants to develop an apartment complex by your house, you don't need to get burned during a negotiation.

Negotiating can be dangerous, or it can be an opportunity for developing and enhancing relationships and yourself. If you let myths determine what negotiation is, then you create dangerous situations where people get hurt and disagreements don't get solved.

To become a successful negotiator, you must first examine the myths surrounding negotiation.

Facts About Negotiation

Preconceived ideas about what negotiating is or should be keep you from getting involved in the process. Sometimes fears keep you from continuing to negotiate when the process gets complicated or difficult. Let's look at what negotiating is and is *not*.

A question follows each negotiation fact. The answers can be found in the following chapters.

1. Negotiating is not always neat or nice.

Often, negotiating takes more time than you planned and can consume more of you emotionally or intellectually than you're willing to give. So you come away disappointed or annoyed because you have to "give" so much for what you get in return. When you accept the fact that negotiating isn't always pleasant, you can dig deep inside yourself to keep working toward the prize you want.

What can I do to keep my perspective when negotiating is not easy?

2. Negotiating is not a game, and it is not a war.

In the pretend world of game-playing, you have rules and you know what it takes to win. You have dice to throw and moves to make. There are risks and rewards. In real life, however, you encounter many complex variables you can't control. It's important to realize that both parties bring innumerable ideas and strategies to the relationship that may change as the negotiating process evolves. Negotiating is fluid. The rules, risks, and rewards change constantly throughout the process. There's no room for inflexibility in negotiating.

What can I do to understand that negotiating is a process?

3. Negotiating is not about winners.

It's about being satisfied. The term win-win is an appropriate outcome of successful negotiating. When you negotiate, you want to win. However, when you negotiate successfully, *your ultimate goal is to come away knowing that both parties had their needs met as fully as possible.* This sometimes means adjusting and reframing your needs. You may not get the original outcome you sought. However, you can come away satisfied with the results when you don't get everything you want. All parties should come away with their needs satisfied and able to talk and negotiate with each other again.

What can I do to create mutually satisfactory outcomes?

4. Negotiating is not about egos.

It's about cooperation. Negotiating is working together. It's about leaving the process with a better relationship.

It's caring about others. It's dealing seriously with the people in your life. It's acknowledging others' emotions, communicating, and accepting them. It's not "eye for an eye." It's not expecting reciprocity from others. It doesn't hinge on agreement. It's accepting the other person even when there are differences. It's not manipulative, and it's not being a pleaser. It's a process for dealing with differences.

What can I do to learn about the differences in others?

5. Negotiating is not about perceptions.

It's about attitude. Understanding another's thinking is the challenge when you negotiate. Whenever you negotiate, you settle a dispute over the differences you have with others in the way you perceive the world. Unless you put yourself in the other person's shoes, you won't negotiate successfully. Negotiating with the attitude that you want to understand the other person will create a positive approach to the process, even though you may believe that your view is the "right" view. When you look at other people's views from their perspectives, you relate to them better and can change your attitude about the way you negotiate.

What can I do to improve my attitude?

Why Negotiate?

As we said earlier, negotiating doesn't occur in a vacuum. It happens in the context of relationships. The context for negotiations contains different and at times divergent history, values, interests, and strategies. Negotiation is a path toward resolution in a conflict, but it's not the only path. You also could try litigation, violence, and sheer abandonment. So how does negotiating help you? Negotiating is a process that helps both parties share ideas, information, and options, while they seek mutually acceptable outcomes.

To make negotiating productive, both parties decide that:

- They can get something through negotiations they can't get outside of it. By sharing ideas, information, and options they can reach an agreement that works.
- They have the resources (time, money, people, skills) to attempt negotiation.
- They want an equitable outcome. Productive negotiations rarely occur between parties who have no trust or commitment or who have no expectations of future relationships.

A negotiation may have one of the following outcomes:

- Win-win: a joint agreement on specific action by both parties.
- Lose-win, win-lose: a joint analysis, with no specific joint action taken and each party operating separately after the process ends. These independent behaviors affect future relationships and outcomes.
- Lose-lose: a total collapse, with each party going forward independently and probably with hostility.

Each of these outcomes has associated costs and benefits. This book will spend much time looking at these outcomes through the prism of relationships, communication, shared needs, and differences. All these issues are important to becoming a successful negotiator.

Fundamental Elements of Negotiating

The goal of the negotiator is to arrive at an agreement. This agreement comes out of a joint problem-solving process. The agreement must include the interests of both parties. Research has shown that joint problem-solving is often the most satisfying way to reach agreement. For that to happen, fundamental negotiating elements must be present:

Trust. Negotiators use the word "trust" to pose the questions, "Can I trust the other side?" or "Can the other side trust me?" Trust is the standard we use to judge the strength of the relationship between the parties.

Process. Process provides the context for building a better relationship and a shared sense of confidence as the negotiation process unfolds. The negotiating process can be broken down into two parts: preparing to negotiate and the negotiation itself.

Preparing to negotiate includes: understanding others, understanding self, understanding appropriate behavior, and understanding strategies.

The negotiation itself includes: the process of negotiating, the environment for negotiating, the data for negotiating, and evaluating outcomes.

Communication. Information flows back and forth between both sides. When that doesn't happen, the negotiation process breaks down.

People. People problems can cripple the negotiation process. These problems may include:

- Emotions—anger, fear, bitterness, vengeance, distrust, worry.

- Miscommunications—not talking, not listening, misunderstanding.
- Misperceptions—different role expectations, cultural variations.

Interests are a key element in the negotiation process. Interests are generally defined as basic needs, wants, or values both parties hold.

Mutual gain is the desired outcome in negotiations. While brainstorming fosters creativity, being controlling or judgmental inhibits creativity.

Bargaining power. Although often seen as the ability to take advantage of the other side, bargaining power as defined in this book is PAK (power, authority, and knowledge)—a positive characteristic that helps both parties win without hurting each other.

Alternatives. If both parties are open-minded and will entertain various alternatives, then finding a win-win solution is more likely.

Criteria for evaluation. These relate to values, desires, and needs. It's important to know what criteria each party brings to the negotiation table.

We'll explore each of these elements in greater detail later in this book.

To collect the tools you need to become a successful negotiator, use the checklist that follows as you move through the book. By the end of the book, you'll have covered all the elements included in the checklist.

Negotiation Checklist

With whom am i negotiating?

- ❑ Who are the parties?
- ❑ What are their needs?
- ❑ What are their personalities/styles?
- ❑ What are their differences?
- ❑ What do they want?

What are the key issues?

- ❑ Do all parties clearly understand the issues? What do we have in common?
- ❑ What do I want? My needs?
- ❑ What am I willing to give?

What is the negotiating environment?

- ❑ What kind of space: public/private?
- ❑ What kind of pressure for decisions?
- ❑ Whose space are we in?
- ❑ What commitment and trust exists?
- ❑ What costs are involved?

What is the negotiating process?

- ❑ Who asked for the meeting?
- ❑ Who will begin the process?
- ❑ Who will set the ground rules?
- ❑ Do we need complete agreement?
- ❑ How are decisions made?
- ❑ Can I promote interest-based negotiations?

What information do i need for negotiating?

- ❏ How will I gather data?
- ❏ Will the information be acceptable?
- ❏ Do I discuss it before the negotiation?
- ❏ Do I need more time to gather data?

What is my negotiation strategy?

- ❏ Do I know my alternatives?
- ❏ Do I understand the problem?
- ❏ Do I know my interests?
- ❏ Do I have a bottom line?
- ❏ What are my goals in the relationship?
- ❏ What PAK (power, authority, knowledge) do I bring to the table?
- ❏ Do I know a good solution and options?
- ❏ Do I have information about the other party?

How will the agreement be reached?

- ❏ Written agreement?
- ❏ Oral agreement?
- ❏ Formal or informal?
- ❏ Do I need feedback from others?

How will the agreement be implemented?

- ❏ Who is responsible?
- ❏ What is the time line?
- ❏ Are additional meetings needed?
- ❏ Does the solution need to be monitored by someone else?
- ❏ Is there a need to renegotiate?

Summary

Negative beliefs often burden your ability to negotiate well. *Negotiation is resolution of a disagreement, using give-and-take within the context of a particular relationship.* By understanding how to create positive negotiations and squelch the myths surrounding the process, you can make everyone involved a winner.

As you read on, keep in mind the following key issues we discussed in this chapter:

- Negotiating is not always neat or nice.
- Negotiating is not a game, and it is not a war.
- Negotiating is not about winners.
- Negotiating is not about egos.
- Negotiating is not about perceptions.

Understanding that negotiation doesn't mean confrontation will help you reach your win-win goal. Negotiating is a good way to resolve conflict. It's not the only way, and it requires trust, communication, and a belief in the process. It takes preparation and an understanding of the process while you negotiate. It requires an understanding of yourself, others, relationships, and differences. The checklist on the previous pages will help you anticipate and prepare for problems and opportunities.

Chapter 2

Understand What Drives You and Others

What Are Our Important Needs?

In a negotiation, you're driven by beliefs and feelings. The ideal outcome of negotiating is a win-win situation with both parties satisfied; therefore, you must know about yourself and others to negotiate that solution. If one or both parties feel they got shortchanged, then it's a win-lose or lose-lose outcome.

Needs are all-important in understanding how to negotiate effectively. Psychologists and behaviorists like Abraham Maslow and B.F. Skinner tell us everyone has three higher needs. After we've taken care of the basics like food, clothing, shelter, safety, and security, we care about these higher-level needs in our life:

- To be loved and valued.
- To be in control.
- To have sound self-esteem.

These needs affect your ability to negotiate well. They also affect what you ask for and what you're willing to accept.

Love and Value

When key people in your life give you affection and responsiveness, it produces positive feelings. If you regularly get these messages of value and love at work and at home, you're more likely to perform better in the workplace and give more of yourself at home.

Love and value statements, such as "I really appreciate your jumping in and helping us finish the board of directors presentation despite your own heavy workload," send positive messages that create positive behavior. Conversely, a steady stream of negative comments, such as, "You're not very helpful around here! We were all in a crunch yesterday, and you left early!" spurs negative behavior.

Knowing that feeling unloved or unvalued causes conflict can help you understand yourself better and negotiate more powerfully.

Control

A second need is to be *in control* of your life: making decisions, determining outcomes, being in charge or having it "your way." Some people call the need to be in control "power." Most people feel good when they're in control because they have the power to influence the behavior or decisions of others. When you negotiate, you often have a mental picture of how you'd like the situation to unfold. When events happen that don't fit this mental picture, you often feel you've lost control.

But being in control 100 percent of the time is impossible. *A key part of being a successful negotiator is recognizing that you can have control in some areas yet not in others.* Learning to respond appropriately to how much control you have in a given situation is crucial to healthy, successful negotiations.

Recognizing that a "control issue" is creating conflict helps you examine yourself, get the issues in perspective, and behave in positive ways to keep negotiations on track.

Self-esteem

Liking yourself and who you are is important. When you don't meet your own expectations, you can feel like a failure. When you don't get what you want, you might blame yourself. It's too easy to use "all or nothing" thinking and over-generalize your shortcomings.

When you go into negotiations with low self-esteem, you often don't prepare to win; rather you prepare to become the victim and see yourself as the loser in the negotiation.

Learning to like yourself in spite of your mistakes brings true self-esteem. Self-esteem means celebrating your uniqueness regardless of your shortcomings, negative events, or the hurtful comments of others. Successful negotiators possess high self-esteem.

Example: Teddie lost a contract with a consulting firm. It was her sixth such loss in the past five months. She was starting to lose confidence in her abilities. As Teddie entered her negotiation for a potential contract with the next firm, she realized that regaining her sense of self-esteem was essential to obtaining the contract. She was determined to show her abilities and talents to the prospective employer. At the same time, she reminded herself that her employment didn't define her personal identity. She would not let self-esteem become a negative issue for the next contract negotiation. By redirecting her thinking, she got the contract.

Your needs can either block or help you during a negotiation. When disagreement arises in negotiations, your hot-button can get pushed, and emotions boil up. It's important to understand the role your needs play in these situations so you can rise above your emotions and stay objective while negotiating. Unfortunately, sometimes you may choose emotional behaviors that damage any chance you might have at negotiating successfully. In this section we'll look at the real reasons people get so emotional.

What Creates Emotions?

When you negotiate, emotions come into play. If the negotiation is going well, you generally have feelings of elation and happiness. When you're getting what you want, you're satisfied. However, throughout a negotiation you often *don't* get the response you'd like. When that happens, it's easy to let emotions rule your response. You may become angry, frustrated, threatened, anxious, or fearful. These negative emotions get in the way of your ability to negotiate well. At that point you react at an emotional rather than a rational level.

The following model illustrates how emotions affect your behavior. The model addresses the three important dimensions of effective negotiating: needs, emotions, and behavior. It's easy to see that both your secondary and primary emotions are driven by the needs you want met: *value, control, and self-esteem.* When you believe those needs are not being met, you're likely to become emotional. When you react emotionally, you might *retaliate, dominate,* or *isolate.* When you understand yourself and your needs, you can choose to *cooperate*. To choose appropriate negotiating behaviors, you need to first identify exactly what needs are not being met.

Model for Understanding Emotions and Behavior

UNMET NEEDS	EMOTIONS	BEHAVIOR/ACTION
Value	Fear/Anger	Retaliate
Control		Dominate
Self-esteem		Isolate
		Cooperate

Behavior Choices

Unmet needs correlate directly to your reaction or behavior during any negotiation. The Emotion and Behavior Model indicates the behaviors you choose when your needs go unmet and your hot-button has been pushed. You might choose to:

1. Retaliate. Retaliation is "getting even" when someone treats you in ways you dislike. When you don't feel *valued* or in *control,* you often become dissatisfied and blame the other person for "making" you feel diminished, out of control, or powerless. No one can "make" you feel any emotion. That's your choice. Blaming others for your problems or lack of well-being is a form of retaliation.

   Retaliation in a negotiating situation almost always guarantees a win-lose or lose-lose outcome. To avoid retaliation, it's vital to identify and deal objectively with the emotional issues (or unmet needs).

2. Dominate. Domination is behavior that results from a need to control or feel powerful. When people believe they are powerless or lack control, it's human nature to want to regain that power. Domination is a behavior that *demands* you get power or control.

   In a negotiating situation, trying to dominate others when they're willing and able to work with you will quickly derail communication. People who try to dominate fail to recognize that in a negotiation, control comes through creating options, maintaining good communication, and continually being able to define win-win outcomes that satisfy all parties. Recognizing that you don't need to have control all the time lets you choose domination when it's appropriate. (Dominance will be discussed in greater detail in Chapter 6, in the section, "Sweaters of Negotiating.")

3. Isolate. Isolation is being separate, away from others. You may sometimes isolate yourself or withdraw when you don't feel good about yourself. A direct correlation exists between low self-esteem and the need to isolate oneself.

   Effective negotiating requires participation, not isolation. Encouraging others to join the negotiation requires an understanding of their needs and emotions.

4. Cooperate. During a negotiation, cooperation results from understanding yourself and others. When you recognize your emotions and needs, you can then choose to behave in a positive way.

Cooperation doesn't happen accidentally. It's a conscious decision. You choose to behave in a way that lets both parties be satisfied with the negotiation. This happens when you understand:

1. Why you are negotiating.
2. What both parties need.
3. The importance of making positive decisions about your behavior.

An integral part of making these choices requires that you reframe your needs and emotions.

How to Reframe Needs and Emotions During Negotiations

You can prepare yourself to negotiate better when you "reframe" what has happened to you and how you feel. Reframing means to look at something in a new way. In this case, it means looking at a situation from a different perspective and seeing it in a positive, productive way. This involves asking questions about feelings and events. Then it's easier to choose better behaviors, because you're calmer and understand yourself and others better. Reframe a situation by asking the following questions:

1. Has this happened to me before?

When problems arise it's important to ask whether you're complicating a negotiation because you're projecting events of the past onto this situation. If so, you make the negotiation much more difficult because you assume the result will mimic previous outcomes. We fail to address the specific problem in its unique context.

The more an event repeats, the more intensely we tend to react. The first event doesn't create the hot-button response. Having the situation repeat itself does. The adage "it was the straw that broke the camel's back" applies here. (While it's important not to make assumptions when you encounter a situation or problem you've faced before, you still need to objectively assess whether your behavior is creating the recurring pattern.)

2. What kind of commitment exists in the relationship?

You're more satisfied when both parties commit to the relationship. You want others to communicate that they are committed to you. When the other party shows less commitment than you do, that tells you they don't value the relationship, and your hot-button gets pushed.

3. What else is bothering me?

This is the "kick the cat" syndrome. Sometimes other problems are bothering you, increasing your stress level, and impairing your ability to negotiate well. If you feel out of control in one area of your life, then when something else goes wrong, you have trouble handling the new problem. Seeing each event as unique is essential to being an effective negotiator.

4. What do I stand to lose if I don't get what I want?

Putting the negotiated event in a larger picture can give you a proper perspective. You can weigh the long-term consequences of not getting what you want. Are you at risk? Will you be hurt physically, emotionally, financially, intellectually? If so, is the hurt survivable? Can you cope if you never get what you want in this case? Often, not getting what you wanted results in the discovery that the loss did you less harm than you feared. Putting problems in perspective helps you remain calm, so you negotiate better. You are no longer frantically seeking to have it your way.

Who Owns the Problem?

You need to ask yourself: "In this negotiation, who is creating the difficulty, and what can I do about it?" Asking this question will help determine if the problem causing the stumbling block spells danger or opportunity.

This negotiating question has four possible answers:

1. The other person owns the problem.
2. I own the problem.
3. There is no problem.
4. We own the problem.

The other person owns the problem. When the problem belongs to someone else, you can do little to change that behavior. You can change yourself, but you have no control over the behavior of others. Taking on responsibility for another's behavior is a dangerous task. You get caught up in an unhealthy scenario that you can't control and that results in a lose-lose negotiation.

I own the problem. An example of this is the professional woman who continually complained to her family about the house's condition when she returned from work-related trips. She would go from room to room discovering unmade beds, unwashed dishes, dirty clothes on the floor, wet towels everywhere, and a family generally unconcerned about the condition of the house. She would yell and scream, and the family would rush around and clean up.

One evening, her husband talked to her quietly. She began to realize that the problem was hers. She knew exactly how she wanted the house to look, and when she returned it didn't meet her expectations. She'd lost control. To get that control back, she yelled so that family members would run around and get the house clean.

When she realized that she didn't have to control the house while she was gone or when she returned, she changed her behavior. Once she did, the family could sit around the kitchen table and agree on an appropriate neatness level for the house. Remember: You can't let yourself be the problem in a negotiation.

There is no problem. Sometimes you create a problem because you wear your feelings on your sleeve. In this case you seek conflict under every rock and make a mountain out of a molehill. Here's an example:

Jane was a new employee at an advertising firm. She gave her first ad campaign proposal, and it was rejected and criticized. Jane soon believed that everyone at the company disliked her, and she started looking for a job elsewhere. She experienced "all or nothing" thinking. Because her supervisors and co-workers had criticized her in one area of her career, she believed they didn't value her. With the help of a friend, she realized she was creating a problem where none existed. With this in mind, she took the criticism of her colleagues, created a better proposal, learned, and grew in her career.

Sometimes we create imaginary problems where none exist. In that case, you may find that the most important person to negotiate effectively with is yourself!

We own the problem. This is the healthy answer to disagreements. When both parties own the problem, each can negotiate with the others to solve it. When you order a steak well-done at a restaurant and the waiter serves it rare, you share the problem. You are an unhappy customer, dissatisfied with your steak. The restaurant prepared the steak incorrectly and didn't give the service it advertises. You must tell the waiter how unhappy you are to get a response. The waiter must return to the chef, express your unhappiness, and have the steak cooked longer. Both parties need to participate in this negotiation for both to be satisfied.

When the answer to the question, "Who owns the problem?" is "We do," you're set to work toward a winning solution. When the answer is "I do" or "They do" or "There is no problem," then the problem must be taken care of *outside* the context of the negotiation. While the problem may come to light during the negotiation, it can't be handled as part of the process. You need to isolate the issues to make sure you deal only with those you can mutually solve in the negotiation. Issues that belong to individuals must be handled elsewhere.

Emotional Barriers to Negotiating

Three key emotional barriers can bring a negotiation to a halt. They are:

Hot-button response. Disagreement triggers your hot-button. It happens quickly and gives you very little response time. For that reason you need to be prepared to stop, breathe, and ask yourself if you're letting emotional barriers block your negotiating. That's why it helps to count to 10 before you speak or to walk away for a moment to cool down before discussing the issues. While it may seem hard to calm down in a difficult situation, you can do it if you prepare yourself ahead of time. Exercising this type of control gives you tremendous negotiating power by positioning you to initiate alternatives that will produce a win-win outcome.

Blame-bag response. The blame bag means letting past memories hinder current situations. You can identify this response by asking, "Has this event happened to me before?" If the answer is "yes," then recognize that the memory of the event is bogging down the negotiation. The blame bag's repository of past harmful memories creates a time bomb waiting to explode in the present.

A good example of a blame bag is when you hold a grudge against someone who has hurt you in the past. Some people take this outlook one step further and hold a grudge against everyone just because one person hurt them.

Particularly in a negotiation, you need to dump the blame bag so the heaviness of the memory won't cripple your judgment or behavior. Another problem with hanging on to the blame bag is that smaller, insignificant issues get bigger. You create larger problems from smaller ones when you haul the blame bag around. Getting rid of the bag is crucial to effective negotiation and handling disagreements in a healthier way.

Dance response. This is when you "dance" or continually debate your negotiations without moving toward a profitable resolution. You concentrate more on the process than on the issues. How does this dance escalate? It escalates when you don't handle problems as they crop up.

When you identify why problems escalate and learn how to stop the process, you control your emotions when you have disagreements in negotiations. When you realize that an emotional response is stifling your ability to negotiate well, you need to address the problem directly, like this:

- Define the problem. In this first step you might say, "When you arrived late to our meetings, it indicated a lack of commitment to the project and a lack of concern for my time." You have just *defined* the problem and focused on it, not on the other party as a "difficult person."

- Share your feelings. You could say, "I felt angry, afraid, and frustrated when...." Here you describe *the feelings* the incidents produced. You use 'I' statements. You don't say, "You make me so mad!"

- Tell what you want or prefer. Then, state what you *want* by saying, "In the future when we work together, I need respect, commitment as a team member, and punctuality." State your request specifically so the other party has a clear understanding of what you want.

- Suggest the outcome that will follow. Tell the positive *consequences* of how behaving in that manner will benefit the other party: "When we both do this, we'll work better as a team, produce better results, and have less pressure throughout our meeting." Don't say, "And if you don't do this, I will never be able to work with you again!"

When you negotiate it's important to:

- Express your feelings objectively.
- Attack the problem, not the person.
- Build relationships as you negotiate.
- Create a positive environment, not a negative one.
- Problem-solve in a positive way.

Disagreements don't have to escalate. When you understand the dance of emotion and follow the guidelines for positive behavior, you work on relationships while you improve your negotiations.

Summary

By looking at the fundamental desires for value, control, and self-esteem, you can understand why you react so emotionally in situations that require negotiation.

The three most important higher-order needs are:

1. To be loved and valued

2. To be in control

3. To have sound self-esteem

Emotional responses are a normal, natural reaction when these needs go unmet. However, emotional responses often stem from fear of the worst possible outcome—which may never happen. When you understand your needs and the reasons for your emotions, you can negotiate productively by choosing appropriate responses.

You can choose your behavior when negotiating. When you respond emotionally you often choose incorrect, unproductive behaviors. Behaviors you may use include:

- *Retaliation:* Getting even and getting back at someone.

- *Domination:* Insisting on control or on being the decision-maker.

- *Isolation:* Withdrawing and being by yourself.

- *Cooperation:* Working with others toward a win-win solution.

Your success as a negotiator depends on choosing the appropriate behavior. Doing so not only gives you control of the negotiation but also enhances your self-esteem. Cooperation in negotiation is the behavior that creates a win-win resolution.

Asking four questions helps you reframe, look at healthy options, and regain value, control, and self-esteem you may believe you have lost. The questions are:

1. *Has this happened before?* (You react more emotionally when a situation repeats.)

2. *What kind of commitment exists in the relationship?* (When the commitment isn't equal, you generally become more upset.)

3. *What else is bothering me?* (Outside factors often contribute to your conflict and emotional response. A negative factor may hurt the negotiation.)

4. *What will I lose if I don't get what I want?* (Place the problem inside the larger scheme of life and get some perspective on it. You may see that you can survive the outcome if you don't get what you want.)

By discovering who owns the problem in a negotiation, you can isolate the issues and deal with them appropriately. When you ask who owns the problem, the possible answers are:

- They own the problem.
- I own the problem.
- There is no problem.
- We own the problem.

The healthy response is: We own the problem.

Recognizing the potential for escalation in a conflict and knowing how to prevent it will keep you on track toward a winning outcome. The *blame bag* hauls negative memories to the present. Getting rid of the memories and blame makes you healthier in negotiating.

By understanding how to block escalation, you can avoid overly emotional responses and negotiate better.

Chapter 3

Learn to Celebrate Differences

Building Healthy Relationships

When you negotiate, you ask for something within the context of a relationship. For that reason, you need to clearly define your relationship as you negotiate. You need to understand where others are coming from and where you stand in your life. Regardless of whether the negotiation is short-term or long-term, when it takes place you still must deal with the relationship that exists at that moment.

Relationships vary over a lifetime. Because of those changes, your negotiating needs also change. You move through different types of relationships with people as you grow and mature; therefore, you negotiate for different outcomes as you grow and mature. This growth cycle affects the nature of your negotiating, so you need to identify your growth cycle to understand how it affects your outlook during a negotiation. The growth cycle you experience throughout your life can be described this way:

Relationship Cycle

Dependence	Independence	Interdependence
("I can't do this *without you.*")	("I can do this *myself.*")	("I want to do this *with you.*")

Ultimately, the goal for the adult in relationships and negotiating is *interdependence*. Negotiating is defined here as both parties being satisfied. I win when we both are satisfied. That relationship is defined by the person who says, "Of course I can do this myself, but I choose not to. I choose to do it *with* you. I know life is richer and more rewarding when I give myself to you and you give yourself to me." Creating harmonious relationships, both casual and intimate, throughout your life defines a healthy person emotionally, intellectually, and spiritually. These interdependent relationships occur in the workplace, the community, the home, and elsewhere. They become a style of interacting with others that lets you live a more rewarding and profitable life. Therefore, you negotiate with the goal of win-win, where we both contribute our ideas, desires, and capabilities for satisfaction with all parties, not just ourselves.

A visual analogy of interdependent living is the "wave" you may do at ball games. Sitting in the bleachers or stadium, you jump up, throw your arms in the air, and yell "Whoo" with hundreds of others. The overall effect is a "wave" of people cheering the athletes as they play. It's a large, effective gesture because so many people do it together. It's fun to watch and fun to join. You don't do the wave by yourself. If you stood up, threw your arms in the air and yelled "Whoo" by yourself, you'd look ridiculous. Yet when we "wave" together, we have an impact on the stadium and the players. So it is with interdependence.

The three possible healthy relationships you have in a lifetime, then, are: dependence, independence, and interdependence. These three relationships also show in your negotiating style. You ask for different things and negotiate differently depending on your relationship stage. When you embrace one of these relationships at the appropriate time in your life, you consider yourself to be operating in a healthy way. When you embrace an interdependent negotiating style, you negotiate in a healthy way.

Sometimes, you find yourself negotiating in relationships with others who exhibit unhealthy behaviors and negotiating styles. Negotiating becomes destructive because you are participating in unhealthy relationships. What are the types of behaviors that result in unhealthy negotiating?

Dependence

Regardless of their ages, some people believe they can't take care of themselves or their problems. This shows in their negotiating approach. They let others solve problems for them and blame others for their lack of satisfaction. *A person negotiating in an unhealthy, dependent way may place the burden of the winning outcome solely on the other person.* A person may say to others: "Do this for me, I can't do it myself." You probably know someone at the office or in your personal life who seems to need someone else to do something they could do themselves. It's easy to get frustrated with a person who is overly dependent and want to tell them, "Get a life! Grow up! Take responsibility for your part of this outcome." The problem is that these people haven't experienced independence, nor do they have the ability to manage their lives, let alone experience the give-and-take required of interdependence.

This type of person is tough to negotiate with, because winning means that you take the responsibility for the outcome while they make false accusations and take no action. You end up pulling them through the negotiation.

Independence

Another behavior that causes unhealthy negotiating is *independence*. People locked in independence haven't developed the ability to work well with others and want to live their lives alone, their way. These people might be difficult to work or live with because they always prefer "doing it their way." They tend to negotiate in a one-sided way too.

A successful negotiation for the person who stays in the independent stage means, "I get it my way all the time, or I am not satisfied." Some adults who have been married five times or switch jobs constantly still say to others, "Leave me alone, I'd rather do it myself." In negotiating they take full responsibility for resolving the conflict and wrongly assume they have all the answers. They may avoid negotiating and move ahead to make decisions without involving others in the negotiating process.

These people are difficult to negotiate with because they avoid working with others in the process. They can't make an appropriate commitment to various relationships, whether with co-workers, employers, family, or friends.

Co-dependence

Another unhealthy behavior and negotiating style is *co-dependence.* Halfway between dependence and independence, the co-dependent develops. Typically, co-dependent behavior begins during the formative ages of 2 to 7, when a child is busy communicating to the world what he is like. Sometimes when a child interacts with the world, the world reacts by saying: "Oh, we like what you are. You are so beautiful, talented, smart, and lovable." When this happens, the child's self-esteem blossoms and grows. As a result, he'll probably develop a positive attitude toward life, others, and himself. This child is growing into a healthy adult!

However, the opposite can happen when this child tells the world what he is like and the world says: "Oh, no, we don't want you that way. You must be as we want you to be." In response to others' rejection of his newfound self, the child develops a "facade" self and believes his real self has no worth. He depends on the world and others for happiness. When this happens, the child rarely experiences independence (let alone interdependence) and sidetracks from dependence into co-dependence.

The co-dependent relies on others (rather than himself) for happiness and manipulates people to behave according to his standards. Co-dependents expect others to live up to their expectations. They are negative, critical, controlling, manipulative, typically tired, and don't listen to others.

Co-dependents are difficult to negotiate with. They enjoy getting involved in negotiations because they get the chance to grandstand and manipulate the negotiating process. Co-dependents may attack a person rather than address the issues, criticize others' opinions, sidestep the issues to dramatize their emotions, and perpetuate the conflict rather than seek resolution. Ultimately the co-dependent negotiator spurs the need to continue negotiating rather than seek an appropriate outcome. Psychologists say co-dependents may be addicted to the momentum of unresolved conflict and need to experience unresolved negotiations. Their control lies in the ability to throw a wrench into the negotiation process and keep it from being resolved.

Interdependence

Interdependent behaviors include honesty, openness, confrontation, acceptance, and empowerment of oneself and others in a negotiating situation. *Interdependent behavior calls for acceptance of others as they are, unconditionally, rather than making judgments based on their performance.* When I give my unique self to you and you give your unique self to me, we accept each other and create a better negotiation process. People who follow an interdependent life style negotiate in a healthy way, because winning does not mean "I get it all my way."

Negotiation Success Through Empowerment

How can you negotiate in a more powerful way? What is the key ingredient to successful negotiating? One strategy that can create successful or unsuccessful negotiating is simply *empowerment.*

Empowerment is a key word in negotiating. When you empower others in the negotiating process, you share the power to make suggestions or decisions or to determine the process used. Empowerment is the essence of building healthy relationships and negotiations. When you empower others, you give rather than take away. It's an attitude about interaction with others. An employer might say to an employee, "I will support you in any way I can so you can make the best decisions on this job." The employer is saying, "I care about you. You are credible with me. I support you and will work with you to accomplish our goal." How can you use empowerment successfully in negotiations?

Follow three steps:

1. Make the decision to empower.
2. Communicate empowerment.
3. Recognize that feelings stem from behavior.

Negotiating can work better when you decide ahead of time to empower the person you're negotiating with. Doing so changes your notion of what winning means and your perceptions of the other person, because you decide to be positive about that person and the negotiations.

Negotiating with the Four Gifts of Empowerment

Adopting empowerment takes a conscious effort. Like any other sort of behavior modification—exercising or dieting, for example—changing your outlook involves self-discipline. Change means teaching yourself new habits, which entails four steps:

1. **Choice.** Recognize that we all have individual choices about how we live our lives. Don't expect others to live up to your expectations, and appreciate the different choices others make. We have differences in gender, race, culture, creed, educational level, and personality type. Therefore, in negotiations you don't let differences become the issue; instead you look toward what you have in common. You find the common ground and negotiate from that perspective.

2. **Knowledge.** Gain as much information as you can about another person or situation so you're more prepared to negotiate. For example, you might find out whether a person is creative or methodical, or whether he likes to work slowly or quickly. The more you know about others' desires and needs, the better you can understand and deal with them.

3. **Practice.** Practice helps you improve the process of communicating and negotiating with others. The skills required to be a good communicator and negotiator take ongoing practice so you'll have a fine-tuned technique at your fingertips.

4. Involvement. Invite the ideas and opinions of others when you negotiate with them. When you ask people to get involved, they feel important and valued. That increases their desire to negotiate a win/win solution.

Recognizing that you have choices about your beliefs, standards, and life style reduces conflict. Creating choices lets you negotiate more effectively, because you don't expect others to live up to your expectations. When you work hard to learn about others and share yourself with them, you gain information about the relationship and negotiate better. When you practice understanding and accepting others for who they are, you strengthen your ability to negotiate even more.

Summary

You negotiate better when you build healthy relationships, whether long- or short-term. As you mature, you evolve through three relationship stages:

1. Dependence: I need you to do this for me.

2. Independence: I can do it myself.

3. Interdependence: I work along with others.

Those same stages show up in negotiating. You evolve as you mature and can negotiate in a stronger way when you build healthy, interdependent relationships. This requires interdependent behavior, including giving yourself to others and accepting others' uniqueness. Interdependent behavior means empowering others.

Co-dependent behavior is characterized by controlling, manipulative tactics that come from low self-worth. This behavior marks a person's need to seek gratification and happiness from others rather than from himself. Codependents have trouble negotiating because of their desire to manipulate and "get things their way."

Empowerment is the way to build better negotiations. Empowerment means extending yourself for the mutual benefit of yourself and others. To experience empowerment you need to follow three steps:

1. Make the decision to empower.
2. Communicate empowerment.
3. Recognize that feelings stem from behavior.

There are many differences among us. Celebration of others means combining empowerment behavior with an understanding of other people's differences. To become an effective negotiator, you need to develop your ability to respect others' differences.

When you recognize that you have choices about your beliefs and standards and learn as much as you can about other people, you boost your ability to be a successful negotiator.

Chapter 4

Negotiate With Honor, Knowledge, and Understanding

How You Speak Means More Than What You Say

Consider the adage, "It's not *what* you say but *how* you say it that makes a difference." Nonverbal behavior directly affects the negotiation process. People "listen" to body language. When body language and words don't match, people place more value on body language. Negotiations can fail or succeed based on the message you send through body language.

Communication specialists report that 93 percent of our communication comes through body language. That means that words account for only 7 percent of our communicating power. Therefore, it's crucial to understand body language so you can communicate your intended message as you negotiate.

Body language includes:

1. Voice pitch (how high or low the voice sounds).

2. Intonation (emphasis placed on certain words).

3. Gestures (the way your hands, arms, and legs move).

4. Eye contact (looking at someone directly or indirectly).
5. Proximity (how close to someone you stand or sit).
6. Facial expression (a smile or frown).

Body language communicates:

1. How much *power* you believe you have in a situation.
2. How much you *like* someone.
3. How *responsive* you are to someone.

Your body language may send a message that supports or contradicts your words; it can help or hinder the negotiation process. Let's say you're talking to an employee about her poor job performance. Two different body-language scenarios communicate different messages:

Scenario No. 1:

An employee comes into your office and you ask her to be seated. Then you stand over her, cross your arms, and look down at her. In a stern tone, you say, "You are a highly valued employee, and I want to talk to you today about your performance on the job."

You've shown that you feel you're more powerful by standing over the person. You've conveyed no warmth or responsiveness by crossing your arms, and your voice tone indicates displeasure and dislike. Although your words weren't negative, the message your body language sent has ensured that negotiations will go badly.

Scenario No. 2:

An employee comes into your office. You shake her hand, smile, and ask her to be seated. You then sit beside her, lean forward with your arms uncrossed and say in a caring tone, "You are a highly valued employee, and I want to talk to you today about your performance on the job."

You've indicated warmth, responsiveness, and little desire for power over this individual. Leaning toward her shows interest and friendliness. Smiling and shaking hands say you are responsive. Your tone says you like the person. Your body language has opened the door to effective negotiation.

A good way to remember the importance of body language is to use the technique "SOFTEN." You can soften the conflict or negotiate better with others when you SOFTEN yourself.

Using "SOFTEN" as a Negotiating Technique

S-O-F-T-E-N is an acronym for:

S: Smile. When you smile at people you send a message that you care about them. Smiling helps erase negative feelings toward others. The smile has been used since prehistoric times to tell strangers we won't harm them. A smile is one of your best tools to send an immediate signal that your purpose is not to do harm. (Note that smiling too much for too long indicates falseness.)

O: Open. Open body posture. When you put your arms behind your back (as opposed to folded in front of you), you appear more relaxed and accepting of others. Another open posture is arms loose at your sides, palms open and standing face-to-face, which indicates responsiveness. Crossing your arms or holding them tightly to your body makes you seem closed off and unresponsive. And turning your back is the most closed posture of all.

F: Forward lean. When you lean toward others instead of away, you communicate interest and willingness to listen. Proximity sends a message of liking and responsiveness. So when you sit in a chair beside a person you're talking with, leaning slightly toward her shows you care about what she says. Leaning away, turning your back or turning to your side indicates you're only partially interested in the conversation.

T: Touch. A handshake, a squeeze, a hug (when appropriate) or a pat on the back all indicate you care about someone. *The appropriate touch in the workplace is the handshake.* The handshake communicates interest and responsiveness in an acceptable way. When appropriate, a pat on the back may accompany the handshake. This type of casual touch sends signals that can reduce conflict or bolster negotiations when words don't seem to work.

E: Eye contact. When you make eye contact with others, you say you are trustworthy, believable, and responsive. When you look away from others, people believe they are not important to you. Refusing to make eye contact may also indicate that a person is not telling the truth or has something to hide. If you disagree with someone and look out the window while she talks, you send a signal that you're not interested in her. When she asks questions and you refuse to look at her, you suggest that you have something to hide. *Always make* eye *contact when you negotiate.*

N: Nod. Nodding your head shows you are listening and processing the conversation. Frequently nodding can be confused with: agreement, so supplement the nod with affirmative comments when appropriate. Nodding also nurtures the conversation and encourages the speaker. It tells others that you are responsive to them. Nodding too much is confusing, however, and you can come away looking silly.

You can use the SOFTEN technique throughout negotiations to show the other person you care about her as you negotiate.

4 Ways to Communicate Effectively When Negotiating

Your communication behavior is important when you negotiate. Letting others know you care about them reduces tension and pumps up your ability to negotiate well.

Here are four ways to improve your communication throughout negotiations, which will help you forge a win-win outcome.

Be clean

Whenever you negotiate, make sure the message you send is the one that you intend. Strive to make your verbal and nonverbal behavior send the same message. Remember that it's not what you say, but how you say it that matters.

Be comprehensive.

Do your homework and know the subject. Know the "who, what, where, when, why, how, how much, why not, and what if." If you negotiate without researching your issues, you can't be effective. Research the other party's position or complaint, too. It's easier to propose workable options if you understand the other person's key issues.

Be calm.

This is easy to say but hard to do. To effectively use the techniques in this book, you need to establish and maintain objectivity throughout your negotiation. That means setting aside emotional responses. That's not to say you should ignore verbal abuse or false accusations. However, it's vital that you remain calm and deal with the issues objectively. When one or both parties lose their tempers or get emotional in a negotiation, at least one party ends up losing.

Here's a behavior-modification exercise that may help you focus on remaining calm:

> *Before you enter into a negotiation, place a rubber band tightly around your wrist. Pop it. When the rubber band bounces back, it will hurt. This serves as a reminder not to lose control while you negotiate. Snap the rubber band whenever you feel frustrated, tense, or exasperated. Each time the rubber band pops and hurts, the reminder to be calm will come to mind. So if you anticipate a difficult situation, discreetly wear a rubber band. (In some situations this technique can distract or even appear neurotic to the other party, in which case pinching your wrist will accomplish the same thing.)*

Be caring.

Communicating in a way that lets others know you care means listening and giving them time to talk. One-sided negotiating is doomed to failure. Understanding others is more important than being understood by them. Listening is honoring the other person. You can avert many dangerous conflicts when you close your mouth and open your ears.

The old saying, "You have two ears and one mouth, so you should listen twice as much as you talk," is good advice for caring about others.

Avoid Escalating Words

Psychologists and sociologists have concluded that some words are "red flag" words. These words upset people quickly. Since your goal in negotiating is to come to agreement and resolution, you need to avoid words that make others negative and resistant. Here are some escalating words to avoid:

1. **"You."** This simple pronoun, when overused, is the same as pointing a finger at the other person. That's why 'I' statements are so important when you negotiate. Studies have concluded that the more a person uses the pronoun "you," the more upset the other person becomes. So structure your sentences with comments like, "I prefer that we have a calm conversation" (in place of "How dare you yell at me?") or "I feel angry when this happens" (in place of "You make me so mad!").

2. **"But...."** This conjunction is negative. It negates whatever came before it and automatically sours the negotiating process. If you say, "You are a valued employee, but I want to talk to you about your tardiness on the job," you've negated the positive statement you made to the employee about being valued.

   If you substitute the conjunction "and" for "but," you'd say, "You are a valued employee, and I want to talk to you about your tardiness on the job." This statement gives equal value to both phrases and doesn't negate what was positive.

3. **"Can't."** Your grandmother told you never to use this word, and she was right. "Can't" implies failure, which means that a person won't change. When you say to another person, "I just can't understand you," you imply that you'll never understand the other person. This makes any attempt at negotiation appear hopeless.

4. **"Always" or "Never."** Generalizations like these imply that something happens 100 percent of the time. "You're always late to work. You never show up on time." But rarely, if ever, is a person, thing, or fact "always" or "never." You exaggerate when you imply that something is that way. Almost everyone dislikes being on the receiving end of an "always/never" accusation. Avoid these two words when you negotiate.

5. **"Should have" or "Ought to have."** The family of "would," "should," "ought," and "could have" demands that people perform to satisfy your standards. (Remember our discussion on co-dependents?) When you say, "What you ought to do is this," you're being manipulative, preachy, and bossy. Can you make much headway negotiating when you're busy telling others what to do?

Communicate Your Preferences for More Effective Negotiations

Now that you know words that upset other people during communication, what can you say to improve negotiation and work toward a positive resolution? The best approach is to communicate your preferences honestly and fairly. Instead of criticizing the behavior of others, spend your negotiating time communicating your preferences as clearly and concisely as possible. Here are three phrases to communicate preferences:

1. "When ... happens, I ..."
2. "I prefer that ..."
3. "Because of ..., I ..."

You might say, "Rather than scream, I would prefer that we speak to each other calmly, because I want to stay on the topic we were discussing." That's a lot better than saying, "Stop that screaming at me before you make me do something we'll both regret!"

By staying calm while you state your preferences, you've established guidelines for negotiation. You're not making allegations or escalating the conflict. Stating preferences is an honest way of staying in control. Also, you're not letting the other person rob you of your self-control.

In the following negotiation scenarios, the first line (in italics) describes the situation that's occurred, and the phrase below it is an example of an appropriate response.

Scenario:

When someone starts to cry:

"I would like to take a short break because I want us to be composed while we have our discussion."

When someone screams at you:

"I prefer that you speak in a softer voice because I can listen to what you have to say better."

When someone threatens to walk out:

"I prefer that you stay because you and I have something important to talk about."

When someone attacks your authority:

"I would prefer that we concentrate on the issues rather than the person because that is what we are trying to resolve."

When someone asks for something that seems unreasonable:

"I would like you to give me more details because I want to understand the reasons for your request."

These phrases work well during negotiation for three reasons. First, they don't include the escalating words that tend to excite others ("you," "but," "can't"). Second, they help you focus on the problem instead of the person. You're not attacking, you're stating your preferences.

Third, you're not concentrating on feelings alone. While your expression of feelings is important, sometimes those feelings may interfere with the other person's recognition of what you seek. This technique lets you express, in a logical fashion, what you prefer, rather than how you feel. When everyone stays calm and focused, negotiations are likely to be successful.

Summary

When you negotiate with honor, knowledge, and understanding, you recognize it's not just what you say but how you say it that makes a difference. Your body language is important.

Body language communicates 97 percent of your message. Body language also communicates:

1. Power.

2. Liking.

3. Responsiveness.

Body language takes the form of:

1. Gestures.

2. Facial expressions.

3. Eye contact.

4. Proximity.

5. Voice pitch.

6. Voice intonation.

S-O-F-T-E-N is a good way to remember the rules to good body language communication:

Smile

Open

Posture

Forward lean

Touch

Eye contact

Nod

When you communicate effectively you become a better negotiator. Hints for better communication during negotiating are:

1. Be clear.

2. Be comprehensive.

3. Be calm.

4. Be caring.

Avoiding escalating words will smooth negotiations. Escalating words are :

1. You.

2. But.

3. Can't.

4. Always/never.

5. Should/ought.

Making 'I' statements lets you communicate your preferences in positive ways that move you toward winning resolutions.

By improving the verbal and nonverbal ways you communicate, you can improve your success at negotiating. Successful negotiation requires successful communication.

Chapter 5

Do Your Homework Before Negotiating

Preparing to Negotiate

Getting ready to negotiate means studying up, priming yourself to be as informed as possible when you enter into the negotiation. It means preparing mentally and emotionally to understand the other person and yourself better. To get ready, you need to understand the motives of others, avoid assumptions, know the specifics of the subject being negotiated, and focus on the main interests of each person. You make the decision to work toward a "win-win" solution during this preparation time. The outcome of your negotiation is largely determined by the attitude of winning you take into the negotiation process.

This chapter focuses on preparation before negotiation and also provides principles to use during the negotiation. Equipping yourself with these principles will help create a successful event.

Know Yourself

This is called self-reflection or self-evaluation. Questions to ask yourself include:

- What do I want out of this negotiation?

- How am I likely to behave?

- What will trigger my hot-button?

- Do my requests fit who I am and what I want in life?

- Are my expectations realistic for this situation?

Evaluate the real reasons you are negotiating. Is what you seek consistent with your moral and ethical code? Does asking for it give you more of what you want from life? Can you live decently if you don't get it? These questions will help determine the reasons for your negotiation. They'll also tell you what you're willing to settle for. If what you want is extremely important, then what issues will trigger your hot-button? Is it self-esteem, value, or control? If others disagree with your moral and ethical code (this may be the reason for your negotiation), then how much are you willing to compromise? At what point will you not be able to compromise?

Then assess how you'll behave when the negotiation is complete. Be prepared for a positive or negative outcome. Ask yourself:

- How will I behave if I get what I asked for?

- How will I behave if I don't get what I'm asking for?

- What am I willing to settle for?

Visualize how much good will come to you if you get what you want and feel your reactions. Then ask yourself what will happen if you don't get what you want and picture your reaction. What alternatives could satisfy you?

Then determine your bottom line for compromise. Visualize what will happen if you must walk away with no negotiated outcome.

Reflecting on these questions means taking a hard look at your intellectual and emotional capabilities. For instance, intellectually, what are you willing to do, ask for, or receive? Emotionally, how will you feel if you win? Or lose? Listen to yourself as you answer these questions. Take the time to know yourself and your motivations for negotiating.

These steps will help you prepare, understand yourself better, and communicate to the other party:

1. Prepare a list of alternatives that you find acceptable. Have your options clearly in mind so you don't feel trapped.

2. List your *interests*. Don't be confined by rigid positions. You may be surprised to find that your interests can be met in different ways by different people.

3. Gather support material that can help explain yourself and your needs to others.

Know Others

Analyze the personalities of the others who will be negotiating. Try to determine or anticipate their key interests and how they will approach the negotiation. This means asking the same types of questions about the other person that you asked yourself. In some cases you can explore the others' needs and motivations by direct questioning. However, in cases where tension exists at the outset of the negotiation, direct questioning won't be possible. In those cases, you'll need to listen to the spoken and unspoken needs the other party is signaling. (Unspoken needs may be indicated by issues that trip the other person's hot-buttons.) Compare this information with the person's current and past behavior and you should be able to put together a picture of his motivations.

If someone is willing to talk, then actively *listen* to him. Ways to listen actively are:

1. Limit your own talking. Listen more than you talk.

2. Be interested and show it. This includes body language that communicates liking and responsiveness. Remember SOFTEN.

3. Tune in to the other person. Concentrate on that person and nothing else. Notice his facial expressions, tone of voice and how feelings are expressed. Let him know that he is important.

4. Ask questions for clarification. Ask these questions sincerely, but don't interrupt the other person. Ask for more details, feelings, how he wishes to accomplish something, or why it is important to him.

5. Hold your fire and don't jump to conclusions. Staying calm and not overreacting to others' thoughts helps you keep a clearer perspective.

6. Listen for ideas, not just words. Sometimes red flag words distract us. Your reaction may stifle what the person really meant.

7. Turn off your own worries. Wanting to be understood or thinking of what you're going to say next can interfere with your listening.

8. React to ideas, not the person. Separate the person from the problem and its solution. Everything else the: person has done to or with you must be separated from his ideas for the negotiation.

9. Get feedback. Ask questions when you speak, so others have the chance to tell you how they feel. Phrases like "Do you ever feel this way, too?" encourage conversation.

10. Notice nonverbal language. Be alert to what the other party communicates and what nonverbal feedback you give him.

Another good way to learn about the other party is to ask other people. They can fill you in on experiences that may relate to your situation. Check other sources such as publications, reports, advertising, speeches, budgets, planning documents, and other items that might tell you more about the person or organization.

You can use two types of questions to gain information about what your negotiating counterpart needs. Type-one questions are open questions, those that cannot be answered "yes" or "no." Questions that begin with "why," "what," or "how" produce open-ended information. Statements like, "What do you think?.... Tell me about ...," "Why weren't you satisfied with...?" and "Tell me more about that..." give the other person a chance to talk and be specific. Use open questions to learn what you need to know about your counterpart. Listen carefully to the answers.

Type-two questions are closed questions that must be answered "yes" or "no." You can use these questions to pin down the other party.

Examples of closed questions are:

- "Would you agree that ...?"
- "Do you still think that ...?"
- "Shall we meet on Tuesday to finish this up?"

These can be used to get a commitment from the other person and to test where he stands. When he responds with a "yes," then you know you're on the right track and can proceed. When he says "no," find out why. Go back to the open questions and keep probing until you feel you can test again for a "yes" or "no."

Getting as many "yeses" as you can establishes points of agreement in the negotiation process. It builds momentum toward a win-win resolution. Don't assume that the other person agrees with you. Test the agreement and get several "yeses" before you give something he will probably disagree with. Getting "yeses" helps you see what you have in common.

Example: You've worn a pair of jeans for only two weeks. They're wearing badly, and you want to return them to the department store where you bought them and either ask for your money back or get a new pair of jeans.

First, check the department store's return policy. Have the documents you need when you return them, then check any guarantee advertised by the company that made the jeans. Maybe the store won't refund the money, but the factory will. Know something about the salesclerk who sold you the jeans. Is he the department manager? Does he have decision-making authority? Will you need to go above him to a supervisor?

Knowing this information gives you an idea of where to start and how to proceed if you aren't satisfied.

Ask the salesclerk specifics he can answer with "yes" or "no," and build the "yeses" by asking the questions that will result in a "yes." Because you've done your homework, you'll be able to ask the right questions!

Avoid Assumptions

It's important to avoid negative assumptions about others, especially regarding their beliefs, values, attitudes, and behavior.

Often you think you're ready to negotiate and fail to do your homework because you assume you have the information needed to negotiate successfully. As in the scenario above, you could assume that the department store had a return policy that would accept the jeans. You'd go in with no other strategy or information and be alarmed to discover that the salesclerk wouldn't accept the jeans because the store had no return policy. You could become angry, thinking you had no other alternatives because your initial assumption was wrong.

Avoid assuming that another person is out to harm you just because he's on the "opposite side" during the negotiations. Because each of you asks for different things doesn't make either party "all bad" or "all good." Generalizations cause trouble by perpetuating false assumptions.

Focus on Interests

Even though you've concentrated on understanding what drives yourself and others, your primary objective is *to focus on the interests of the people involved, not their position.* If the salesclerk refuses to refund your money, that's his position. His interest might lie in adhering to the department store's rules or preserving his commission based on selling a certain number of jeans. Focusing on interests means you go back to what motivates people to ask for what they want. So, if you can help the salesclerk meet his interests (sales commission, not violating the store's policy), you can request an exchange in place of a refund for the jeans.

It helps to ask what the other person's interests are, then listen to the answer. Simply asking the other person, "What is your primary interest?" or "What are you most concerned about?" helps both parties focus on interests. It may take several questions and careful listening on your part to understand the reason for the other person's position.

Use these four good steps to understand interests:

1. Ask for the objections. Encourage an open dialogue, making sure that nothing stands between you and your goal at the close of the negotiation. Ask non-threatening, open questions. For example:

    • "What problems do you foresee in my returning these jeans?"

    • "Is there anything else I need to do to get my money back?"

2. Listen to the objections. Avoid the impulse to jump in and overwhelm the other person with your feelings or thoughts.

3. Acknowledge the objections. Instead of arguing with the objections, keep the dialogue open by acknowledging them. Saying "Um-hmm" or "That's certainly a consideration" shows you are listening and receptive.

4. Classify the objections according to main categories. That way you can deal more easily with the objections. Examples are:

- *Smoke-screen objections* are phony objections that hide real issues. You can judge whether someone is hiding issues by looking for lack of eye contact or irrelevant objections. Be polite and keep probing.

- *"Knee-jerk" reactions* are usually given for the sake of objecting because many people think they need to have lots of objections when they negotiate.

- *Emotional objections* come when people feel threatened or disliked. Don't take emotional objections personally. Listen, keep the dialogue upbeat, and probe for more information by asking questions.

- *Real objections* are the objections that will form the heart of your collaboration. You need to take these into account for the negotiation to reach agreement.

Once you've heard the others' objections, you know what stands between you and your goal! Be prepared to follow these principles when you go into negotiation.

Creating a Successful Event

A successful event is a resolution that is win-win for both parties. When both parties win, both get their interests met. The desire for a win-win outcome must be clear in your mind before you go into the negotiation.

Like other events in your life, you're in charge of your attitudes and behavior. A person's attitude determines the outcome of an event. So, when you decide the outcome will be win-win, you choose winning assumptions, feelings, and behaviors when you negotiate. A step-by-step process of how you decide to negotiate and then implement the negotiation looks like this:

Step One: You are *dissatisfied.*

Step Two: You want to be *satisfied* (WIN).

Step Three: You want the other party to be *satisfied* (WIN).

Step Four: You choose *winning feelings* about yourself and others.

Step Five: You choose winning *assumptions* about yourself and others.

Step Six: You choose winning *behaviors.*

Step Seven: You have winning *outcomes.*

Any time you negotiate, you go through these steps. When you choose a win-win solution you make positive statements and actions. When you choose to lose you make negative statements and actions. You have four choices for outcomes, and only one means a winning outcome for both parties. Your choices are:

1. Win-win: I win and you win. We both are satisfied. With the win-win choice, both parties leave the negotiation with a level of satisfaction that makes the next negotiation possible.

2. Win-lose: I win, you lose. I am satisfied, you are dissatisfied. Win-lose puts the winner in a "let's do this again" mode, but the loser may say, "I haven't finished the last one yet. You may win this battle, but I'll win the war." An angry workforce revolts.

3. Lose-win: I lose, you win. I am dissatisfied, you are satisfied. The lose-win puts me in a position to seriously question if this was worth the effort, saying, "Now that I've lost, do I ever want to try again?" A dispirited workforce can easily be the end result of lose-win.

4. Lose-lose: We both lose. We both are dissatisfied. Lose-lose means both parties walk away, often unemployed, almost always unempowered and in every instance questioning the worth of even trying.

Ultimately, when you embrace a winning attitude, assumptions, and behaviors, you have winning outcomes. The reverse is also true. In other words, you decide whether you win or lose. You are in charge of the outcome.

You can go through each of these seven steps and create negative, unsatisfactory outcomes for yourself and others, or you can create positive outcomes. The outcome is determined by your attitude and decisions. When you win, it's because you make an effort to win. When you lose, it's because you created losing outcomes. (Note: Sometimes others are bent on creating losing outcomes for themselves and everyone else. We refer to these people as "difficult." Chapter 7 will help you turn losses into wins.)

Mentally Preparing for Success

Once you've decided to create a successful event, you need to prepare for it mentally. This is called "self-talk." Self-talk helps you assume a positive attitude because it programs you to behave in a productive fashion. When you self-talk positively, you generally behave positively. When you self-talk negatively, you often behave negatively.

Self-talk can move you from negative thinking to positive thinking and ultimately to positive behavior. How does this happen? Positive self-talk is one of the best tools for overcoming past failures.

Your brain is a miraculous device. Like a large computer, your brain takes in information, files and stores it for immediate and future use. Your brain stores and uses whatever you program it to receive. Like a computer, the brain doesn't care what information we store. Because the brain has no system of discerning whether a fact, thought, or emotion is right or wrong, true or false, it stores every word you speak or action you take. You, in turn, make decisions based on what you've stored in your brain. If you've stored negative, exaggerated, or distorted information, then you have incorrect data to use in making decisions. If you've stored positive, accurate, and targeted information, then you have correct data that will help you make sound decisions. The key to making good decisions, particularly in negotiating, is the "input" to your computer or brain.

How can you improve the way you program yourself? First, you need to understand how you operate as a human, and second, you need to understand how you can use self-talk to improve your programming activity.

Our Behavior as Humans

First, it's important to look at why we behave the way we do. Our behavior choices stem from our experiences, beliefs, attitudes, and feelings. These come largely from our experiences. At any point in our lives we are the culmination of a variety of experiences that have produced our unique beliefs, attitudes, and feelings. Our behavior is the direct result of these experiences, beliefs, attitudes, and feelings, especially in situations that may involve conflict, tension, or negotiation.

By analyzing each area that affects your behavior, you can understand ourself better.

1. *Programming:* The application of your experiences.

2. *Beliefs:* Images about yourself, higher order, others, life.

3. *Attitudes and feelings:* The bridge between beliefs and ehavior.

4. *Behavior:* The manifestation of programming, beliefs, attitudes, and feelings.

Programming

Your life has been molded by your experiences, by what others have said to you and by what you've said to yourself. These experiences have been positive and negative. You've chosen to keep and record some of the experiences; you've chosen to leave others behind. You are the product of the positive and negative programming you've been exposed to. Negative programming often causes negative behavior, so if you want to erase the negative behavior in your life, an appropriate tool is self-talk, which helps replace negative with positive behavior.

Beliefs

Your beliefs arise from your programming. According to psychologists, we have certain belief structures we use to develop our lives. These structures are notions about life, higher order, ourselves, and others. Throughout your life you've been exposed to programming that's helped you determine what you believe in these four areas. For example, you might say:

- Life: "I believe that life is great and deserves celebrating" or "I believe that life is terrible and unfair."

- Higher Order: "I believe that God exists and is personal" or "I believe that God does not exist and doesn't make a difference."

- Self: "I believe that I am strong and worthy" or "I believe that I am a loser and will never win."

- Others: "I believe that people are good and deserving" and "I believe that people are evil."

Attitudes and Feelings

Just as your programming determines your beliefs, your experiences generate attitudes and feelings. You might say, "I love life... I love myself... I love God... and I love others." Or you might say, "I hate life... I dislike myself... I reject God... and I ignore others." With each of these statements you express an attitude or feeling about your beliefs.

Behavior

Your behavior is the action you take toward yourself and others. Behavior is affected by experiences, beliefs, attitudes, and feelings. If they are positive, then you'll likely have positive behavior, and vice versa.

Using Self-Talk to Reprogram Behavior

Behavior is a direct result of programming. To create positive behavior, you need to create a positive program. Therefore, when you decide to negotiate, you can prepare by creating statements that reflect positive beliefs, attitudes, feelings, and behavior. Self-talk can help you do that. Here are the phases, or steps, of self-talk that produce reprogramming:

1. Affirmation.
2. Visualization.
3. Goal-setting.
4. Forgiving and forgetting.

Affirmation

An affirmation is a positive mental statement you make to yourself to provide inspiration. It's saying to yourself, "I did a great job... I'm a terrific person... I am strong and worthy... I am lovable." When you make affirmative statements, you feel better about yourself and the world around you. Using affirmation also helps when you don't get everything you wanted. It can help you avoid feeling like a failure because you didn't get the desired results. For instance, when a particular outcome disappoints you, you might use this affirmation: "I am going to learn from this experience and be more knowledgeable and prepared next time. I am a stronger person because of this experience." An affirmation is also a positive statement you make to others. A wife might say to her husband, "You are a special husband."

The lack of affirmations in a relationship can create the notion that one party doesn't value the other. Simply assuming that others know you care for them isn't enough. Articulating affirmations to yourself and others requires that you speak words to help change thinking.

Visualization

These are mental pictures you create to preview specific actions, behaviors, or outcomes. Visualizations are mental dress rehearsals. You practice what the event will look like and how successfully you'll accomplish it. Athletes, performers, physicians, and successful professionals often use visualization to enhance their performance. You can visualize a successful negotiation and mentally walk through the phases of the process. When you visualize failure and fear that the negotiation will bomb, you set yourself up for failure even before you begin.

Professional skiers preparing for competition were asked how they became so good and how they prepared for the event. They responded that they had a three-part plan. First, the night before the competition they checked the weather report and visualized what the slopes would be like and what they could do to win. Second, the morning of the event they drove to the slopes and visualized again how they would lean into the wind or negotiate the snow. They actually felt the snow and measured the wind. Third, as they skied they followed the plan they'd visualized and kept it foremost in their minds. They never once visualized losing. They always visualized winning in the competition.

Goal-setting

Here you develop a specific plan for your negotiation. Unless you have a plan, you won't know where you want to go. The goals are your road map. Without the road map, you risk getting sidetracked by your hot-button responses. Keeping your eye on what you want rather than on the side issues helps you stay focused. Your goals need to be specific and related to the relationship. They need to demand enough, while not being too extreme or unrealistic. For example, you need to have more elevated goals for your employees than, "I hope they show up on time."

When you set specific goals, you strive to achieve what you want for yourself and others.

Forgiving and Forgetting

This entails leaving your emotional "baggage" behind. This baggage could include bad memories of previous encounters with the other party or recollections of failed negotiating situations. When you forgive and forget, you put the past event behind you and start fresh with the new negotiation. Of course you never wholly forget. What you learn from past experiences helps you in the future. When you forgive the person or yourself for what happened, you change your reaction to that memory. You no longer have a negative perception of the event. The memory may return, but you learn from it and don't respond negatively.

Using affirmations, visualizations, goal-setting, and forgiving/forgetting will help you prepare a positive mindset when you negotiate.

Summary

You need to be prepared to negotiate effectively. You can do this by using the following steps:

1. *Know yourself by* reflection and evaluation.

2. *Know others* by listening and asking.

3. Avoid assumptions.

4. Focus on interests, not positions.

5. Create a successful event by choosing win-win.

You determine the outcome by doing your homework. This entails learning as much as possible about yourself and others. By focusing on interests rather than positions, you can meet everyone's needs. Deciding to win creates an attitude that results in improved assumptions, feelings, behaviors, and outcomes.

Understanding yourself requires that you look at your background and determine why you behave the way you do. The steps to understanding yourself better are found in understanding your:

1. Programming.

2. Beliefs.

3. Attitudes and feelings.

4. Behavior.

By using self-talk, you can reprogram your beliefs, attitudes, and feelings and ultimately change your behavior in a positive way. The four types of self-talk are:

1. *Affirmation:* saying positive things about self/others.
2. *Visualization:* seeing yourself doing the positive action.
3. *Goal-setting:* making a plan for success.
4. *Forgiving/forgetting:* letting go of past baggage.

When you follow these self-talk methods, you create a positive approach to negotiations. This prepares you to work toward a win-win result.

You're in charge of winning or losing. If you decide to lose, then you probably will. The same is true for winning. Here are seven steps for winning:

1. Dissatisfaction.

2. Desire to be satisfied.

3. Desire for others to be satisfied.

4. Choose winning feelings.

5. Choose winning assumptions.

6. Choose winning behaviors.

7. Have winning outcomes.

By using positive self-talk and making the decision to win, you choose winning behaviors that result in a win-win outcome for both parties.

Chapter 6

Negotiate Actively, Honestly, and Fairly

"Do Unto Others As You Would Have Them Do Unto You."

—The Golden Rule

Ways to Negotiate

There are a variety of ways to negotiate, and there is a process of negotiating. When you're clear about various strategies and know what to do when you negotiate, you're prepared to win-win. Everyone will have their own preferences and styles of negotiating. That's why it's important for you to prepare. As we look at ways to negotiate, we'll identify steps to take, styles to use, and rules for fairness and honesty.

In a sense, your negotiating style is as distinctive as the clothes you choose to wear each day. Each time you prepare to negotiate, you select your favorite negotiating "sweater" and put it on. The sweater feels comfortable because you've worn it many times before. It's comfortable because it's your style.

However, when you wear the same comfortable sweater in every negotiation, you gain success only some of the time—not all of the time, because negotiations demand different sweaters or styles for different occasions. Being prepared to win means being ready to wear a variety of sweaters ... and maybe even the layered look!

7 Sweaters of Negotiating

When you decide to win-win, you can use numerous styles or strategies to achieve that outcome. If you use the sweater analogy for negotiating, then there are a variety of "sweaters" you can wear. You don't have to rely on your favorite old sweater. You have a versatile wardrobe available. You can use the following negotiating "sweaters" singly or in various combinations depending on the circumstances.

The sweaters can be divided into two sections: The first four are passive; the next three are active. Passive and active approaches don't mean strength or weakness, but are negotiating strategies. A passive and an active sweater can work well together.

Ignore/deny

When you deny a problem, you spend your energy avoiding it, not solving it. As a rule, it's better to face problems in a negotiating situation. But first you must distinguish the problems that relate to the issue at hand from those that don't. Getting caught up in an irrelevant problem keeps you from solving the more important issue being negotiated. So it helps to have an "Ignore/Deny" sweater handy. Wear it when you need to avoid issues that don't pertain to whatever you're negotiating. But remember not to ignore when you and others are being hurt. It's not good to ignore feelings, and it's not advisable to ignore issues that will surface later. They always come back stronger the second time.

Suppress

This means to bite your tongue. But suppress only for short periods of time. Suppressing for long periods can cause long-term physical and emotional stress. Suppressing is a lightweight, short-term sweater that works well over another sweater. This sweater can come in handy when someone is obviously trying to push your hot-button in a negotiating situation. Let's say the other party criticizes your family or your personal life when neither relates to the negotiation. Don't let yourself rise to the bait. Redirect the conversation by pointing out that those comments don't relate to the issue at hand. Or let a long, uncomfortable pause occur and then pointedly return to the topic being negotiated. But don't suppress when you and others are being hurt. Acknowledge hurtful comments for what they are: vicious, inappropriate, and counterproductive.

Leave

This involves withdrawing or walking away. You can leave in three ways:

1. For a short time and then return.
2. For a long time and then return.
3. Permanently.

Leaving permanently exhausts your options, so always try the least severe approach (leaving for a short time, then returning) first and move incrementally toward walking away from the negotiation altogether.

Examples:

Step 1. Say to the boss: "I would like to think about what you've proposed. Let's talk about this at the same time tomorrow."

Step 2. Say to the boss: "We agree on the basic problem. Let's each work out three or four solutions and meet to discuss them in a week."

Step 3. Say to the boss: "I am leaving this position and choosing not to work here anymore."

You need to measure how much you stand to lose by walking away. If you have a lot to lose, then leaving for a short time or long time and coming back is better than leaving forever. Exhaust all your alternatives before leaving forever. Many people have left careers and retirement benefits on the negotiating table by giving in to their emotions and quitting. Later many wished they'd worked harder using the first two ways to "leave."

As we look at the next four styles of "sweaters," you can use a criterion that will help you decide which sweater to wear. That criterion is the PAK acronym:

- **P**ower.
- **A**uthority.
- **K**nowledge

Power is influence, credibility, and your effect on others. Status in the workplace and placement in the company hierarchy don't matter. A person can have a great deal of influence without having a high position in the company. A company CEO reflected one day on the amount of power she had when she first joined the company as a new CEO. She soon realized that her administrative assistant, Norma, had more influence than she did. Norma knew everyone in the company—their names, spouses' names, children's names, and family history. She could pick up her phone and get anything taken care of because of the influence she had with others. Norma had power! In this case, the company didn't give her power. She claimed it for herself by her credibility and effect on others.

Authority is what the company gives you. This might include the responsibility to hire and fire others, travel, or spend money. When people are surveyed on the job, most indicate that they would like more authority to carry out their tasks. Authority usually comes when a worker rises in the hierarchy.

Knowledge is what you've learned, both formally and informally. No one can take knowledge from you. Formal education gives people professional PAK. When you deal with people, you gain PAK as a "people person."

As a new supervisor, Danielle was having trouble supervising her employees. She knew she'd made mistakes and felt inexperienced handling some of the employee issues. Danielle knew that her boss, Mary, had been a longtime supervisor in another department. She sought advice from Mary because Mary had the knowledge about people and problems. She had PAK.

Placate

This is when you recognize another's PAK. You say, "You appear to have a great deal of experience in this matter" or "This incident must have given you some keen insights." For someone to earn the right to be placated, he must have PAK and want to accept responsibility for decisions. Placate when you are in the other person's PAK area. You may wish to placate to recognize that person's PAK and then move carefully to a second style or sweater after you've built trust and understanding.

When Carla, a human resources representative, planned a welcoming event for the company's new employees, she needed to work within the budget the finance department gave her. While Carla wanted to prepare a more gala event than the budget allowed, she knew her spending limitations were firmly set. She had no other options but to be creative in the use of the budget she received. Carla wouldn't have been wise to demand more money from the finance director. The finance director had PAK in the area of budget. Carla recognized that authority and she placated.

Dominate

Dominance is the sweater to wear when you control an outcome. You can dominate when you have PAK. Dominance is good in crisis. When others don't have PAK and time is short, someone with PAK must make decisions. Don't dominate when others have PAK or when you don't have PAK. The statement "My way or the highway!" may create a war that isn't worth the outcome. When you both have PAK, go directly to compromise.

Denise, a consultant, worked with the director of nurses' training at a hospital. When she finished her needs assessment at the hospital, she phoned the director and said, "I have the answers to your problems. I know what those nurses need, and I'm ready to come and do the training!" Knowing that Denise's dominant style was not very appealing, the director suggested they both look at the needs assessment and together make decisions on what training the hospital needed. In a careful way, the director moved Denise from a dominant style to a compromise. In this case, compromise was appropriate because both parties had PAK. Denise tried to use dominance inappropriately with a director of nurses' training who certainly had PAK.

Compromise

You compromise when you make a 50/50 split in your negotiation. You give half and ask the other person to give half. Compromise is essential when you both have PAK. You both know what to do and have the influence to carry it off. You both win by compromising. Don't compromise when neither of you has PAK. You will be half wrong!

Teddy and Fran both worked on the assembly line repairing the same widget. They both wanted the same lunch hour but were told that the line had to keep running throughout lunch. Teddy and Fran negotiated and compromised by alternating the days they went to lunch at noon. Teddy and Fran had the same PAK and knew that compromise was beneficial for both.

Collaboration

This entails using a team effort at every level. When you collaborate, everyone involved must have PAK. You share in the interests of others at every level of give-and-take. Collaboration works when people have time, commitment, trust, resources, and PAK. Collaboration doesn't work well during a crisis, when no trust exists and when participants don't have PAK.

Let's look again at the example on page 89. Mary, the experienced boss, can help Danielle, the new supervisor, by giving her advice and working alongside her, rather than taking away her authority. Instead of being dominant, Mary chooses to collaborate with Danielle to help her improve as a supervisor.

All these strategies can work for you at the right time. You can determine which sweaters to wear by asking the following questions:

1. Do I have much PAK?
2. Do others have much PAK?
3. Does much trust and commitment exist between us?
4. Do we have much time?
5. Do we have the money or resources?

When the answer to all these questions is "yes," then collaboration is a good choice. If not, you must look at the "no" answers and choose the appropriate sweater from your closet. Let's use Jack and Donald as an example.

Example: Jack worked as a unit manager for Donald's company. Jack knew that the growth in his unit depended on boosting production, and for that he needed more people and equipment. While Jack was in Donald's office negotiating for more help, he discovered that no more resources were available.

As Jack left Donald's office, he started thinking about the strategies he could use to have a win-win for the company and for his unit. He first *suppressed* any negative comments toward Donald. He *left* the office and worked *collaboratively* with his employees to see what recommendations they could give Donald to demonstrate the benefits of giving them additional resources.

Jack returned to Donald and *placated,* empathizing and indicating his understanding of the problems Donald faced if he gave Jack's unit the money. Later he worked with Donald to *compromise* in their plans to give Jack's unit resources.

Jack used a process of negotiating with a variety of sweaters to produce a win-win outcome. Negotiating is a process of continuing to work toward a positive outcome. Not only do you use different styles when you negotiate, you also approach the negotiating event in a positive way. The following steps to negotiation will lead to positive outcomes.

7 Stages of Negotiating

Now that you've decided which sweaters to wear, which words to use, and what homework to do, just how are you going to approach the process of negotiating? On the following pages you'll find the seven stages in the negotiating process.

Define the problem

Don't focus on the other person's position. Rather, focus on her interest. State the problem unemotionally and from the perspective of each party's needs, desires, and fears. You might say, "I have a problem that I need your help in solving. The toaster that I bought from your store last month does not work properly. I know the store works hard to maintain a high level of customer satisfaction, so I am returning it." You did not attack the person. You did not say: "What a lousy store you are to carry inferior product lines." You focused on your mutual interest in the problem, which is customer satisfaction.

Look for what you have in common

Both parties want a good relationship. For the store this means your continued patronage and for you it means getting value for your money. Continue to focus on that. When you keep the focus on mutual interests, you reinforce the reason for the negotiating relationship.

When spouses conflict, counselors ask them to focus on the areas they have in common like their home, children, friends, and experiences. When employees conflict, mediators ask them to focus on their common interests like the customers they serve or the product they deliver.

Realize that multiple interests are involved

For the store, the multiple interests include profitability, repeat business, dependability, and reliability. Find as many factors as you can, then identify the importance of each to you and to the other party. Recognize and acknowledge these mutual interests. It helps to have each party describe them.

Look toward solutions rather than the problem

For example, replacing the toaster would solve your problem. A "loaner" toaster would be acceptable while the store gets yours repaired. Don't focus on the broken toaster. Focus on the solution. Focus on fair, impartial criteria to determine your solutions. Frame each issue with this objective standard. Be reasonable. Listen and encourage (through positive feedback) reasonable thinking from the other party.

Focus on benefits for both parties

As you suggest possible solutions, suggest the benefits for each of you. Ask for input and brainstorm to solve the problem. Let the other party know you're committed to a solution that produces mutual benefits. Do this by suggesting ideas, not deciding them. Involve the other party in generating options, but don't lock anyone into these ideas.

Decide on a time to evaluate and make decisions

This could be the same time tomorrow, next week, in an hour. Keep to the schedule. Commitment by all parties is crucial. Be prepared to dovetail multiple interests into one solution. Describe the benefits the other parties will gain in their solutions and help them decide. Continue reframing their suggestions in light of your own. *Agree on principles, then fine-tune the details.*

Reinforce commitment after you've agreed

Make statements like "I'm glad we've agreed. Now, we've made the commitment to *(describe action)*, right?"

Commitment is a step beyond agreement. It puts everyone in motion to act out the agreement they made. Shaking hands, looking each other in the eye, and smiling usually help reinforce a statement of commitment.

These steps help produce a positive outcome, but they're not always easy to take! You can prepare yourself to use these steps by being principled as a person. Being principled means you are loyal to your beliefs and do what's right for yourself and others. Staying principled takes techniques and practice in six areas.

Stay Principled

Staying principled means staying focused on the *interest* of both parties and *building relationships* as you negotiate. That doesn't mean you manipulate or control. Being principled in a negotiation means remaining true to yourself and doing the best for yourself and others. On the following pages are some ways to stay principled while you negotiate.

- Be honest and forthright. *Don't* give in just so the other person will like you better. Don't be afraid of not pleasing the other person. You may ask for things that others don't like in order to stay honest. Be true to yourself and others.

- Be reliable and trustworthy. Don't radically change what you ask for in midstream and throw the other person off guard. Flexibility is important, but complete reversals in your position confuse the negotiation. Maintain your interests. At the same time, don't expect others to accommodate you because you were willing to compromise with them. Thinking someone else "owes" you and "ought" to give in to your requests is dangerous thinking.

- Be both logical and emotional. Don't let one stance outweigh the other. Emotions are an important part of how you understand yourself and others. You "feel" certain ways, and your feelings can't be ignored. Your thoughts and logic are important also. Reasoning is the rational side of you. Thinking clearly may involve walking away from a negotiation until you've calmed yourself. You can't have a win-win negotiation when you're in the middle of a tantrum.

- Be open in communication. Remember the Four Cs of Communicating: Clear, Comprehensive, Calm, Caring? The better you follow those, the better your negotiations will go. Listen to others and let them tell you what they want. *Understand what the other person wants before trying to persuade her to accept what you want.* Listen more than you speak. Remember, your body language helps you communicate more positively as well.

- Be accepting of others. When you appreciate the differences between people, others know you're not judging them, and they are more likely to accept you. Put yourself in their shoes and understand their needs. Intolerance of differences causes misunderstandings that frequently stir up conflict. We are different and we have different needs. Accepting different needs is the first step toward finding solutions in negotiation.

- Be persuasive. Use your best skills to convince others that what you seek is important to you. Convince the other person that your needs are meaningful. When you communicate the importance and *reasonableness* of your needs, you are being persuasive. *An essential part of being persuasive is to communicate how meeting your needs also helps the other party.* Show how what you seek will benefit the other person. Always find the importance for others in what you want. Don't control or manipulate.

Summary

In this chapter we've discussed seven ways to negotiate, using the "layered look" to achieve a win-win outcome for both parties. When you combine active and passive "sweaters," you can be flexible and effective in achieving your outcomes. The seven sweaters of negotiating are:

1. Ignore/deny.
2. Suppress.
3. Leave or withdraw.
4. Placate.
5. Dominate.
6. Compromise.
7. Collaborate.

PAK is an important characteristic to recognize when you negotiate because it influences the types of sweaters you might wear. P-A-K stands for:

Power   Authority   Knowledge

The negotiation process has seven steps:

1. Define the problem.
2. Look for what you have in common.
3. Recognize multiple interests.
4. Look toward solutions rather than the problem.

5. Focus on benefits for both parties.
6. Determine a time to evaluate and make decisions.
7. Reinforce commitment after you've agreed.

It's also important throughout negotiation to stay principled, to be true to yourself, and build honest relationships with others. Staying principled means being:

- Honest and forthright.
- Reliable and trustworthy.
- Both logical and emotional.
- Open in communication.
- Accepting of others.
- Persuasive.

You can negotiate in a variety of ways to create a win-win.

Chapter 7

Create a Champion from a Naysayer

What to Do When People Say "No"

Negotiations are not always easy, clean, or nice. Often, despite careful preparation and your commitment to a win-win outcome, the other person doesn't cooperate. Here are ways to handle a situation when someone says "no."

1. Don't take it personally.

The other person's response is a reaction to the circumstances, not to you. When you assume the other person is trying "to get you," you get in trouble. It's easier to stay calm when you don't take the person's resistance personally. The other party probably would have responded "no" to anyone under the same circumstances. Remember that you weren't singled out as the special person to receive a "no."

2. Have "Plan B" and "Plan C" ready at all times.

Propose alternatives as ideas rather than solutions. If the other party says "no," be ready with options. Make sure the ideas highlight the benefits for both parties. Make them the best options you can possibly offer. But don't sell yourself short. Don't "give away the store." Say, "One fair alternative might be..." or "What if we did..." See how you can modify your suggestions. Sometimes a small change makes all the difference toward finding solutions.

3. Suggest a temporary postponement in the decision.

Ask that you not have to accept the other person's response as a definite "no" in order that both parties have more time to think it through. If the other person agrees to rethink, you haven't received a "no" after all. You've received a "Maybe—I'll think about it."

Three Magic Phrases

When negotiations don't get you what you want initially, it's important to thank the other person for his effort, rather than get frustrated and demean the effort. Three magic phrases that often work are:

"I respect..."

"I appreciate..."

"I agree..."

These phrases defuse the differences between you and the other party and convey how you value the other person for participating in the negotiation. What follows the magic phrases is not nearly as important as the phrases themselves. You might say:

"I respect your honesty with me ..."

"I appreciate the time you are giving me ..."

"I agree, we have a problem ..."

Example: Max wanted to enroll in a class at the local college. The course would prepare him for a job that would become available soon. He'd been guaranteed the job if he took the class. But because he enrolled on the last day of registration, the class had no room—and it wouldn't be offered for another year. Max asked the registrar for special permission to enroll in the class. The registrar's response was, "No, if I do this for you, I'll have to do it for everybody." Max knew he needed a "yes," so he said,

- "I agree, you want to be fair with all students."
- "I appreciate your willingness to be honest with me about your policy."
- "I respect how difficult situations like this are for you and the college. But this class is essential for my new job. And I'm taking this job to prepare myself for a better career in this community. I am willing to be placed on a waiting list if you would consider calling me after the first week of classes. A student might have dropped the class. I am willing to discuss this with the instructor, also."

The registrar agreed to put aside his "no" response and to hold a place on the waiting list while Max talked to the instructor. Max knew the dropout statistics and felt confident he would find a seat. He successfully negotiated with the registrar and the instructor to be flexible in meeting his needs.

How to Handle a Difficult Person

Sometimes you find yourself negotiating with people who are intent on being belligerent, controlling, obnoxious, or just plain difficult. We refer to people who behave this way as "professional harassers."

People who are obnoxious and hard to get along with become that way because of weak self-esteem. When people don't feel good about themselves, they often put down others in an attempt to elevate their self-worth. They continue in this downward spiral, setting up a scenario for you to lose, because your loss makes them feel better about themselves. It's important to not let them gain control over your loss in a negotiating situation. If that happens, you can take alternative steps.

Scenario:

Chris worked for Sam. Sam was the manager and Chris was the administrative assistant. Sam was difficult to work with because he frequently criticized Chris' personal life. He harassed him about his private trips and relationships. One day Sam asked Chris to meet in his office to discuss the annual report. As Chris walked into Sam's office, Sam said, "Well, aren't you special coming in here with that smile on your face. I'd smile too if my father bought me a new car." That is harassment. Chris made a mental note that he was not going to tolerate the abuse and implemented the following steps:

Listen to the person

Ask the individual to repeat what he said. Sometimes we are the difficult person, because we fail to hear what someone is saying. Often we accuse others of saying one thing when they meant another because we weren't listening. Saying, "Pardon me, I didn't hear what you said— would you please repeat that?" gives the other person an opportunity to think about saying it again.

Chris said, "Pardon me, Sam, I was taking my coat off and didn't hear a word you said. Would you please repeat it for me?"

Generally, this question will stop a difficult person from continuing. It's just too much trouble to repeat the criticism. The person will say, "Oh, you didn't hear me; well it wasn't important anyway."

In Sam's case, however, he repeated the harassing statements, so Chris continued to Step Two.

Repeat for clarification

"Let me see, this is what I hear you saying *(repeat)*. Am I correct?" Or "Let me ask a few questions, to make sure I have my facts straight *(repeat)*." Or "Please correct me if I am wrong, you said *(repeat)*." All these statements clarify for you and the other party what was said.

Chris used the phrase, "Did you really mean what you said? Because if you did, then this is what I prefer." This nonattacking approach gives Sam time to reflect and decide if it's worth continuing in a threatening way. Most people will stop and clarify themselves. Some might say, "No, that's not what I meant..." Then you can continue with the discussion after you understand what the person really meant.

However, Sam was more difficult. He said, "Yes, that's exactly what I meant. Do you want to make something of it?" Chris moved to Step Three.

Ask for solutions to your problem

Chris might say, "What bothers you about my smile and good mood? Is it inappropriate for work? What suggestions do you have?" This requires Sam to further define his position and forces him to look at solutions. In this case, Chris senses that Sam is probably more interested in being critical than in defining a problem and seeking a solution. Forcing Sam to focus on solutions will either make him understand that the problem lies within himself or, more likely, will make him back off entirely and think twice about making such comments in the future.

Once Sam backs off, Chris might indicate he wants to focus on the annual report, which sets the stage for a productive meeting.

If the behavior or demands are escalating, disengage

Don't be a victim of someone else's threats. Leave the door open for future negotiating. Chris could suggest making an appointment to discuss the annual report another time. He could offer to get coffee to create a cooling-off period. Sometimes a physical disengagement, however brief, is necessary because it gives the parties a chance to change their positions and soften their attitudes. The physical break lets everyone "save face" by releasing the parties from having to give in.

Discuss alternatives to difficult behavior

Talk directly about what is happening and ask what you can do to help.

If a person refuses to negotiate, talk about principles. Chris might say, "Sam, you wouldn't want me to treat you this way, would you? Do you think hearing these comments would make you feel very good?" This approach helps establish principles for negotiating.

Use interruptions to switch subjects or start a new discussion

A distraction can interrupt the negotiation, refocus both parties, and create a better atmosphere.

Three options for interruptions are:

1. Detour.
2. Interruption technique.
3. Broken-record technique.

Detouring involves "leaving" the subject for a moment and returning. Make a joke (if appropriate in the situation), get a cup of coffee, comment on a photograph, suggest a 10-minute break. Detouring and rambling can divert everyone's attention from the barriers that stand between them. The participants can escape to neutral ground. (Note: Detouring and rambling don't work if they appear as an attempt to stall or buy time. In this case, you create greater barriers.)

In Chris' case, an example of detouring would be: "Excuse me, Sam, let me get some coffee for us. Cream or sugar? Why does the coffee here taste so much better than coffee at home?" This gives them time to cool down and count to 10.

Interrupting involves doing something more offbeat or creative. You might crack a joke or tell an amusing story. You interrupt, or use a distraction, to startle the other party and stop the momentum of negative behavior when other strategies have failed. You can suddenly make an unexpected comment or do something outrageous that stops the other person in his tracks. Use caution, though. If your timing is wrong, this approach can splinter your credibility and weaken your negotiating position.

Broken record is when you repeat which behavior you don't want and what you want in place of it. Chris could say: "I don't want to talk about my personal life. I want to talk about the annual report. If we can't discuss the annual report now, it will cause us to miss our deadlines and reflect poorly on both of us."

Keep records

Maintain a log of your negotiations and meetings that details when you met, what you discussed, and what you agreed on. This becomes a reference for your next meeting. When Sam called Chris back and said, "Come meet with me to go over the annual report. That report is due in 10 days, and you haven't discussed it with me yet," Chris could say, "Sam, we've met five times to go over the annual report. Each time we spent the meeting discussing my personal life. Of course I'd like to talk about the annual report. Let's have a meeting and discuss only that."

When All Else Fails

In our imperfect world, not every negotiation ends in a win-win, nor does the difficult person respond to our strategies. Sometimes it seems that no amount of sharing or educating will get you to a "yes." When this happens, you can use two alternatives that work in the same spirit as the win-win negotiation: mediation and arbitration.

Mediation helps when communication and negotiation don't work. A third party gets involved to help both parties reach agreement. The mediator may be the manager, a corporate person, or an outside consultant. The process is usually voluntary and nonbinding.

Arbitration is used when there is pressure to make a decision. A third party listens to the arguments and reviews the evidence, then renders a decision.

Using a combination of negotiation, arbitration, and mediation is referred to as *alternative dispute resolution* or ADR.

Summary

Even though someone tells you "no," you have options. First, stay in control of yourself and suggest alternative behaviors. When someone says "no":

1. Don't take it personally.
2. Have plans "B" and "C" ready.
3. Suggest a temporary postponement.

Certain phrases also help erase a negative or difficult attitude. Dissolve tension by using the three magic phrases:
1. "I respect ..."
2. "I appreciate ..."
3. "I agree ..."

Difficult people put others down because they have low self-worth. You need to protect yourself from this type of person, This step-by-step process works for handling difficult people:
1. Listen.
2. Repeat to clarify.
3. Disengage if threatening.
4. Use interruptions to switch subjects.
5. Discuss options.
6. Ask for solutions.
7. Keep records.

By looking at alternatives, discussing problems for clarification, and asking for help, you can reverse a difficult situation. Even when the other party is being difficult, you can address the trouble directly and keep the negotiation on a principled track. Your final option is mediation and arbitration, identified collectively as alternative dispute resolution.

Chapter 8

Create Satisfaction With Your Outcome

Stages of Satisfaction

Satisfaction has short-term and long-term stages. There is immediate gratification (I get it my way right now), and there is long-term gratification (in the end I got what I wanted). Sometimes you ask for immediate gratification and don't get it. At that point, you have a choice: You can be unhappy and dissatisfied, or you can look at the larger picture.

Satisfaction is a continuum. At one extreme you get exactly what you want. At the other extreme you get nothing you wanted. Most of life falls in between, and so do most negotiating situations. Your job is to enjoy the successes, learn from the failures, and cope with the varying degrees of frustration that lie in the middle.

Sometimes not getting what you sought ends up producing a positive outcome. Days, months, or years later, you recognize that being told "no" forced you to be more creative and make better long-term decisions for yourself. The stages of satisfaction are:

1. Immediate reward: instant satisfaction.
2. Delayed reward: delayed satisfaction.
3. Different reward: adjusted satisfaction.
4. Rejected reward: acceptance satisfaction.

Immediate reward

This means getting what you want immediately and being instantly satisfied. When this pattern of reward behavior continues, you learn to expect instant reward and set yourself up for frustration and disappointment when, in more difficult situations, rewards don't come. Instant gratification is an unreasonable expectation. If you experience it, see it as an unexpected gift. You set yourself up for continual frustration when you believe you deserve immediate rewards.

In negotiating, as in life, you're more likely to get an immediate reward when you've prepared well for the outcome. You believe the goal is attainable, you plan your strategy, and do the necessary work to make it happen. As a result, asking for the "reward" is appropriate and reasonable. Often when you're not prepared, you don't get the reward immediately. Sometimes you wear the wrong "sweater" when negotiating, so you have to wait longer for the results you want.

Scenario:

Jan received a C in English on her report card. She believed she deserved a B because someone else in her class with identical grades on tests and attendance received a B. She met with her teacher, showed her the comparisons, and had her grade changed. Jan's request was reasonable, and she prepared her argument well, so she received an "instant" reward.

Delayed reward

You don't get what you seek immediately; you continue working for it and get it later. While it takes longer because your timing is off, you're satisfied in the end.

In this case, your expectations for instantly getting what you want are unrealistic at the outset, but by readjusting your expectations and working longer toward your goal, you become satisfied. Success in this case takes patience. This is the most typical sequence of events for most of us. Learning to be patient gives you strength in negotiating situations. Often it takes longer than you think to get an answer that satisfies you. Without patience you get exasperated and jeopardize your position by becoming inflexible or combative. You may even give up entirely. Patience is one of your most important tools during a negotiation.

Scenario:

Mark wanted a salary increase and believed he deserved it. He was promised the increase within one year of starting his job. His first anniversary and annual job performance appraisal did not produce the raise. Mark was irritated that he didn't get what he was promised. Before he spoke with his boss, he did some research and found that the company's productivity and sales were low at the time, thus creating a conservative approach to salary increases. When he negotiated with his boss, Mark indicated he understood the company's financial problems, clarified that the original commitment hadn't been tied to the company's performance, and then proposed that his raise be postponed a year but increased to compensate for the delay. His boss agreed. Mark was patient and got what he wanted and deserved.

Different reward

Not getting what you asked for but getting something else is called *adjustment*. In any negotiating situation, you need to recognize the benefits of being satisfied in different ways. The outcome may be better or worse than your original expectations. If it's better, you're even more satisfied. If it's worse, then you need to accept the differences and find satisfaction in the outcome, despite your disappointment.

Scenario:

Nettie wanted the new director's position that was opening at her company. The job would be a step up and mean a higher salary. She worked hard to prove herself to her boss, her colleagues, and the new president. She assembled letters of recommendation, revamped her resume and prepared her interviewing skills. She placed her name in nomination for the position. When the applicants were sorted and the top five chosen, Nettie was number six. Ultimately, someone from outside the company was hired who had the same credentials and background as Nettie. She was upset. She knew she was qualified, yet she felt that because she was "good ol' Nettie," the company hadn't viewed her qualifications objectively.

Nettie decided to apply for a similar position at another company. She got the job and began to grow in her career because of the new challenges she faced.

Ultimately this change will prove a greater benefit to her career than getting a promotion with her previous employer. Why? Because changing jobs demonstrated that others consider her valuable and that she can adapt to new situations and challenges.

Sometimes you get rejected at one negotiation and find your reward elsewhere. Winning doesn't necessarily come from only one place.

Rejected reward

You not only don't get what you asked for, but you don't get anything else from the negotiation. You come away empty-handed. This calls for acceptance. No one finds accepting this type of disappointment easy, but sometimes you have to deal with it. You have two choices. You can create unhappiness for yourself or others and be miserable, or you can admit your disappointment, recognize that you don't like it, and accept the fact that it happened. You then live with that acceptance and move on and find satisfaction elsewhere in your life. Creating acceptance and satisfaction when you don't win is the ultimate growth process in negotiation.

Scenario:

Samantha lost her job as a mechanical engineer. After 18 years of working for a major company, she was out of work and couldn't find a similar job with equivalent pay. She was devastated and wondered what had gone wrong. Over the next year she tried desperately to return to the engineering field and resume her career. Nothing was available, yet she had to keep supporting herself and her family. To earn some kind of living, Samantha went to work at a local department store. Nothing about her situation made her happy initially.

But over the next several years, Samantha began to learn a great deal about herself and why she'd felt the way she did when she lost her job.

Samantha didn't get what she wanted, but she accepted and grew from her disappointments. She readily admits she is a better person today and appreciates life and work relationships much more than she did in the years she was in her fast-paced career. Samantha grew and created acceptance for herself in her life.

Ironically, all four satisfactions can create "good feelings." The difference is in your perception and attitude. Attitude constitutes 90 percent of your acceptance in a negotiation. The other 10 percent is the effort or hard work it takes to change. That means that your happiness and satisfaction level depend 90 percent on your choice of attitude. You can make yourself happy or unhappy.

You can use affirmations to say, "I didn't get what I wanted in the negotiations, but I am not a loser. There are other things in my life that make me happy."

You can use visualizations to see yourself winning in life regardless of the loss you've experienced. You can say, "I see myself being content with where my life is at this moment. I see myself winning in other areas and being happy."

Use goal-setting to make a new plan with new goals, regardless of the setbacks you've experienced. You can say, "This goal didn't turn out the way I expected; however, I learned something, and I'll realize other goals. This experience has made me more knowledgeable, and in the future, other situations will work even better for me."

You can use forgiving and forgetting to let go of past, failed negotiations or relationships and move ahead to improved ones.

Short-term and Long-term Goals

It's important to look at negotiation as a process of obtaining long-term and short-term goals. You don't just negotiate, get what you want, and quit. Each of your many life negotiations is a series of smaller goals that fit into a larger life goal that can be described as "quality of life."

This means you prioritize your negotiations based on the important things in your life: your needs, values, and aspirations. Some negotiations are more important at different times in your life. Sometimes you discover later that a negotiation wasn't as important as you thought. Sometimes you discover that a negotiation was more important than you thought and made a significant difference in your life.

You can nurture your attitude about outcomes in negotiations by:

- Remaining positive.
- Visualizing yourself in adjustment and acceptance.

Staying committed to a positive attitude and learning how to improve who you are and how you communicate are keys to being a good negotiator. Focus, rationality, and flexibility are some of the best tools a negotiator can have.

Summary

Satisfaction with the outcome of a negotiation means different things. The stages of satisfaction are:

- Immediate reward.
- Delayed reward.
- Different reward.
- Rejected reward.

All can result in satisfaction when you adjust your attitude and/or accept the outcomes.

Negotiation is a process. It's not a one-time event. The long- and short-term goals of your negotiations ultimately fit into the scheme of your life goal. Your satisfaction with an outcome depends on its importance in your life plan. It also depends on your attitude and perception. In short, how good a negotiator you are depends on you. How satisfied you are with your outcomes depends on you.

Epilogue

Negotiating is not a mystery. Negotiating is communicating what you want. Negotiating exists within a relationship. You don't negotiate alone—you do it with others. When you negotiate successfully, you communicate what you want in ways that persuade and satisfy others. You understand the other party better and communicate in mutually acceptable ways.

The negotiating principles discussed in this book are techniques you're already familiar with. Intuitively you know how to build better relationships, understand yourself, and know the right things to say or do to create conflict or good vibes. Yet knowing and doing are two different things. And sometimes it's hard to keep doing the "right thing" without being reminded.

The principles we've talked about in this book teach you how to negotiate, build better relationships, and create a healthier self. Using these principles takes practice, and with time you'll continue to improve.

You've completed this book, yet your need to learn about negotiation continues. Because negotiating is a process, your continued work must be a process too. Keep on working to improve. Read more on the subject. Ask questions of others. Ask questions of yourself. Use the questions and principles in this book to become the best negotiator you can be.

A story is told of the famous cellist, Pablo Casals, who was to be interviewed by a young reporter at his studio. Casals kept the reporter waiting past the scheduled time. Throughout the wait, the reporter heard Casals' music coming through the studio's French doors. Finally, the doors opened, and Casals appeared. He realized he'd kept the reporter waiting and apologized profusely:

"Oh, my young friend, I am so sorry to have kept you waiting. You see, I was practicing my cello all day, as I do every day, and I totally lost track of time. I forgot you were waiting."

The reporter jumped to his feet and said, "You are the world's greatest cellist, and you tell me that you have been in your studio practicing your cello all day and that you do that every day. Whatever for?"

Casals turned to the reporter and said, "Ah, my young friend, that is precisely why I practice my cello all day, every day...*to remain the world's greatest cellist.*"

You've improved your negotiating skills by reading this book. You'll continue to improve as you negotiate each day in the real world. Negotiating is an ongoing process. It is not always a singular event. You'll learn from each negotiation that takes place. And as you work at it, you can make your goal *to become the best negotiator that you can be!*

Index